"The

On Sunday mornings, Seoul's noisiest neighborhood enjoyed a brief moment of peace. Before
long, young Korean women in heels and too-short
skirts would slip out of cheap guesthouses and
click quickly to the subway, their eyes downcast
and their wallets a little thicker. The Nigerian peddlers, who sold T-shirts, knockoff handbags, and
marijuana, if one knew how to ask, would emerge,
lugging black garbage bags. Just before the noon
checkout, bleary-eyed GIs would straggle up the
street, stopping for a Whopper or a glazed donut
and then slinging their backpacks over their shoulders and heading back to base.

But before any of this, in the hour or two after
sunrise, there was blissful quiet.

Just after 8 o'clock on March 18, 2001, a high-
pitched cry pierced that stillness.

On the first floor of one of Itaewon's many cheap
motels, a young Dutch woman was screaming as
loud as she could, racing along the narrow hallway,
banging her fists against the plywood-thin doors of
the shabby rooms.

"There's a dead body in my room," she
shouted.

COURT TV
PRESENTS:
MURDER
IN ROOM 103

THE DEATH OF AN AMERICAN STUDENT
IN KOREA—AND THE INVESTIGATORS'
SEARCH FOR THE TRUTH

HARRIET RYAN
FOREWORD BY COURT TV ANCHOR JAMI FLOYD

AVON BOOKS
An Imprint of HarperCollinsPublishers

Court TV Presents: Murder in Room 103 is a journalistic account of the murder investigation of Kenzi Snider for the 2001 killing of Jamie Penich in Seoul, South Korea. The personalities, events, actions, and conversations have been constructed using court documents, interviews, letters, personal papers, research and press accounts. Dialogue in quotes has been taken verbatim from trial and pre-trial transcripts, other sworn statements, and interviews by the author.

AVON BOOKS
An Imprint of HarperCollins*Publishers*
10 East 53rd Street
New York, New York 10022-5299

Copyright © 2006 by Courtroom Television Network, LLC
ISBN-13: 978-0-06-115443-0
ISBN-10: 0-06-115443-1
www.avonbooks.com

First Avon Books paperback printing: October 2006

Avon Trademark Reg. U.S. Pat. Off. and in Other Countries, Marca Registrada, Hecho en U.S.A.
HarperCollins® is a registered trademark of HarperCollins Publishers Inc.

Printed in the U.S.A.

10 9 8 7 6 5 4 3 2 1

ACKNOWLEDGMENTS

Murder in Room 103 would not have been possible without the support of my colleagues at Court TV. The editors at Courttv.com, where my reporting on the case initially appeared, offered unceasing encouragement from the moment I pitched the story until I wrote the last page. Jim Lyons first suggested a book about the case and shepherded me through the publishing process. Catherine Quayle listened patiently to innumerable rants and improved every sentence she touched. Galen Jones provided time and money for me to write. Mark Fichandler arranged financing for my first trip to Korea. In addition to her art direction for the Web series, Stella Min translated documents, answered questions about Korean culture, and put me in touch with her sister, Rose, who guided me around Seoul. Meredith Leiman spent countless hours turning grainy videos into striking photos. Jami Floyd championed this story and the issues underlying it both on-air and off. I am grateful also for the contributions of Brad Dunn, Lori Greene, Benny Lin, Tracy Majka, Matthew McLaughlin, Michael Morenko, Jillian McNamara, and Harry Swartz-Turfle.

I benefited from the patience, support, and prayers of my family and friends, especially Owen and Susan Ryan, Maddy Ryan, Jim Ryan, Irene and Phil Pian, Pat Ryan and Ray Cave, Lisa Fried, Mina Hah and Andy Brothers, and Bryan Lavietes.

Why would anyone confess to murder, especially one committed thousands of miles away and in which there is no evidence linking her to the crime? That is one of the questions Harriet Ryan deftly explores in *Court TV Presents: Murder in Room 103*. The journey on which she leads us is a compelling comparative study of how we solve crime in America and how they do it 6,000 miles away. *Murder in Room 103* reveals at once the tremendous failings of the American criminal justice system and its unsurpassed genius, all through the prism of a brutal crime that happened on the other side of the world.

Americans learn of "the right to remain silent" nearly as early as they learn The Pledge of Allegiance. That right, dictated by the U.S. Supreme Court in *Miranda v. Arizona,* is one of the most well known rules of law ever to have been handed down by the Court.

At the heart of "The *Miranda* Decision," as it has come to be known by virtually every American, is the Fifth Amendment to the Constitution: "No person shall . . . be compelled in any criminal case to be a witness against himself." This includes the right to remain silent at the earliest stages of a police investigation.

The late Chief Justice William Rehnquist was no friend of *Miranda*. He dissented from the majority opinion in 1966 and made no secret, in the years that followed, of his distaste for the decision that estab-

viii COURT TV PRESENTS

lished the police procedures necessary to preserve this right against self-incrimination. Yet even Rehnquist came to accept *Miranda* as part of the American legal fabric. Late in his life, the Chief Justice wrote: "*Miranda* has become embedded in routine police practice to the point where the warnings have become a part of our national culture."

Yet time and time again people confess, not just to petty theft or other nonviolent offenses, but to murder of the most sordid and gruesome variety. They confess in great detail and with seemingly sincere remorse. They implicate others. They outline for police details of the crime scene, the weapon, the murder itself–details "only the killer could know."

Most people who confess to murder are guilty, and most often there is additional incriminating evidence to corroborate their confessions. But some people confess, even when they haven't done anything wrong.

A false confession is counterintuitive and self-destructive–damning and compelling evidence of guilt, even if it is not supported by any witnesses or forensic evidence. A confession that is not true is an exceptionally dangerous piece of evidence precisely because it can single-handedly lead to the trial and conviction of an innocent person.

Yet untold numbers of defendants have given police outright confessions, only to be later exonerated by DNA evidence. These confessions are not prompted by internal knowledge of guilt. Instead, they are sometimes motivated by duress, even coercion. Fear of violence and the threat of a longer prison sentence–or execution–can lead people to confess to crimes they didn't commit.

Ironically, innocent people are more likely to waive their right to silence out of a naïve belief that, because they haven't done anything wrong, they have nothing to fear in talking to police. Memory is fragile, however, and when a person is under the stress of a lengthy and intense interrogation, her memory is vulnerable to suggestion. A young suspect, especially one with no experience with the criminal justice system, may begin to doubt her own memory when presented with false evidence. Skilled interrogators can suggest a false memory and then offer false "facts" to fill in the gaps. When a particularly guileless person's version of events is challenged in this way, what she knows to be true can be upended. The result: an "internalized" false confession.

In *Murder in Room 103*, Harriet Ryan dissects a possible instance of this: a brutal murder and the investigation and various statements, admissions, and confessions that follow. Into that mix, she gently folds a complex layer of cross-cultural confusion and controversy. The result is a riveting story woven from four strands: a chaotic crime scene; the exploitation of sexual angst; international politics; and the bungled investigation of authorities in a faraway place.

This last strand is Ryan's greatest achievement: the unraveling of a classic American murder mystery in the forbidding context of a foreign system of justice and all the implications of that uniquely alien setting for the outcome of the case.

The extraordinary context for this true crime tale is a cheap motel room in a small, far-flung country. The major players are Americans, but when they get caught in these tragic and sordid facts, two cultures–and legal systems–collide: one that retains centuries-old customs and traditions; the other, a world leader in crime scene investigation and analysis.

With an American dead on their soil, police in that distant land are confronted with what is for them a rare occurrence–murder. The authorities scarcely know how to secure the crime scene, preserve evidence, or identify and question witnesses. When international pressure is brought to bear on a case badly managed from the start, U.S. interrogation techniques are exported to a culture where police are more interested in preserving order than disturbing it. Momentary clarity results only to be undone by the very person who seems to hold the key to the truth.

Ryan is most inspired here for she never draws a conclusion about who is guilty. She leaves the ultimate decision as to guilt or innocence to us. Her storytelling is passionate and sympathetic, her research meticulous. Yet Ryan never once gives even the slightest hint of what she believes to be the fact of the matter.

In her objectivity, however, is found a kernel of the truth in this most intriguing case–truth not only about who is guilty of the murder in room 103, but also a higher truth about justice and the uniquely American way we pursue it.

Jami Floyd,
July 2006

CHAPTER 1

GREEN BEER TONIGHT!

March 17, 2001
Itaewon District
Seoul, South Korea

*B*y 10:30 P.M., Nickleby's Pub is packed. Army guys wade through the crowd with pitchers of green beer, pouring for anyone who holds out an empty plastic cup. Speakers blast Top 40, and on a makeshift dance floor, giggling couples in T-shirts and tight jeans grind against each other. From the pool tables in the rear, there is good-natured shouting. Laughter rings out from booths where GIs are hitting on expat school-teachers. A group of exchange students push through the door and take in the rollicking St. Patrick's Day scene. They smile at what they've found: a frat party in the middle of Seoul. The soldiers are raucous and happy. Tomorrow they will be back up north, shivering in some remote base and dreaming of their next leave.

*The conversation is easy and flirtatious: Where are
you from? What are you doing here? Do you want to
dance? There is kissing and groping and a few whispered propositions, but in the exuberant swirl of the
bar, it's hard to take anything seriously.*

*Outside the steamed-up windows, Seoul sprawls in
every direction, massive and incomprehensible. In the
warmth of Nickleby's, though, everything seems familiar and manageable.*

*But undetected in all the carousing, a terrible clock
has started. And with each beat of thumping music
and every belly laugh, one reveler's life is ticking to an
end.*

The old women were up first. They padded out onto
their sidewalks in smocks and slippers to clean away
the broken glass and trash and vomit. At this hour,
Itaewon's streets were quiet except for the low idle of
cabs at a taxi stand. Drivers dozed in their front seats
or stood against their cars smoking. At regular inter-
vals, a city bus glided by a vacant stop.

On Sunday mornings, Seoul's noisiest neighborhood enjoyed a brief moment of peace. Before long,
young Korean women in heels and too-short skirts
would slip out of the cheap guesthouses and click
quickly to the subway, their eyes downcast and their
wallets a little thicker. The Nigerian peddlers, who
sold T-shirts, knockoff handbags and marijuana, if
one knew how to ask, would emerge, lugging black
garbage bags. Just before the noon checkout, bleary-
eyed GIs would straggle up the street, stopping for a
Whopper or a glazed donut and then slinging their

backpacks over their shoulders and heading back to base.

But before any of this, in the hour or two after sunrise, there was a blissful quiet.

Just after 8 o'clock on March 18, 2001, a high-pitched cry pierced that stillness.

On the first floor of one of Itaewon's many cheap motels, a young Dutch woman was screaming as loud as she could.

"There's a dead body in my room," she shouted. She raced along the narrow hallway, banging her fists against the plywood-thin doors of the shabby rooms.

In a few seconds, the hall was filled with other foreigners, all exchange students like the young woman.

"What's wrong, Anneloes?" they asked. "What's wrong?"

Sobbing, Anneloes Beverwijk pointed behind her to the open door of Room 103 and whimpered.

"There's a dead body in my room, and I can't find Jamie."

Another Dutch student, a young man named Jeroen Kuilman, ran to the door, followed closely by an American teenager, Kenzi Snider. Inside the doorway lay the naked body of a woman. She was sprawled on her back with her arms flung out and her legs slightly spread. A black fleece jacket was draped over her head, but the lower third of her face was visible. It was crusted in blood and swollen, and there were cuts and abrasions on her chin and neck. Her shoulders and upper chest were dark blue with bruises. There was no doubt she was dead.

The police summoned to the Kum Sung Motel from a nearby substation took one look at the bloody crime scene and herded the six exchange students into an adjacent room.

The students sat on the bed crying and hugging one another. A patrolman pointed to Room 103. "Who?" he said.

The students shook their heads and shrugged. One of their group, a twenty-one-year-old American named Jamie Penich, was missing, but with the jacket and the blood and the swelling, they couldn't say for sure if the body was hers.

If she has a tattoo on her back, a map of the world, then that's Jamie, one of them volunteered.

The officers disappeared and returned a moment later.

Yeah, that's your friend Jamie, they told them.

A couple of the female students burst into tears. This was not how study abroad was supposed to go.

Two weeks before, they had arrived in South Korea for a semester at Keimyung University, a Presbyterian college three hours south of Seoul by train. The university, just outside the provincial city of Daegu, was beautiful with its hillside campus and Georgian architecture. But the student body was enormous and could be intimidating to outsiders. There were twenty-seven thousand full-time students, only sixteen of whom were foreigners. The international students hailed from Holland, Finland, Russia, Germany, Japan, and the United States, but they clung together like brothers and sisters.

"We lived in the same dorm. We took the same classes. From the second we woke up in the morning to the minute we went to bed, we were together," a student from the University of Nebraska recalled.

Intense friendships developed in hours. Often they were based less on personality and common interest than basic communication. If two people spoke English, they became friends.

During those first two weeks, the students got to know the campus and explored Daegu. With 2.5 million people, the city was large, but it was not especially cosmopolitan. After two weeks of hanging out in Daegu's karaoke bars and nightclubs and watching subtitled movies on campus, some students wanted something more exciting. A group started planning a weekend jaunt to the big city, Seoul.

After the final class on Friday, March 16, six students boarded a train to the capital. There were two Dutch students, a Finnish couple and two Americans: Jamie, a junior from the University of Pittsburgh, and Kenzi Snider, a nineteen-year-old from Marshall University in Huntington, West Virginia. A seventh student, a Russian girl, was to meet up with them Saturday.

Before she boarded the train, Jamie phoned her parents in Pennsylvania to tell them about the trip.

"Don't stay in some fleabag motel. Stay in the Holiday Inn," her mother chided her.

"We will," Jamie assured her.

After the police officer told the group that Jamie was dead, he gestured for them to remain in Room 102 and shut the door.

The students immediately turned to Anneloes, who had shared a motel room with Jamie.

What happened? they asked.

She shrugged and wiped at tears. When I went to

bed, Jamie wasn't home, and when I woke up, she was like that, she said.

Someone turned to Kenzi.

Weren't you guys together at the bar?

Yes, but we came home together, Kenzi said. It was late, but she was fine. I even walked her to her room.

At nineteen, Kenzi was the youngest in the group, but she was the most experienced international traveler. Her father had worked for the U.S. Air Force and State Department and she had grown up all around the world.

Hand me the *Lonely Planet*, she said, referring to the guidebook that is the backpacker's Bible. We're going to call the embassy.

She dialed the number and a switchboard operator picked up.

"We're Americans. There's just been a murder. Can you come and help us?" she asked. Another student dialed one of the administrators in the university's study-abroad office. She had just begun explaining their situation when the door swung open. The hallway was now filled with police officers, and they were not just junior patrolmen.

An older officer was yelling at them in Korean. They couldn't make out the words, but the message was clear: Hang up the phone right now.

In gestures and broken English, the students were told to stand up, leave all their belongings where they were, and quickly exit the motel. Outside, a bus was waiting to take them to the police station. The sight of the bus and white foreigners, some in pajamas, being marched onto it drew the attention of passersby. Staring out the windows, the students saw Itaewon in the harsh morning light. It was a seedy strip of bars, fast-food joints and nightclubs. Every sign was in English, and the stores featured knockoffs of Nikes, Pumas and Polo brand clothes in sizes large enough to fit Americans.

Throughout South Korea, Itaewon was known as a staging ground for foreign partying, especially by the thirty-seven thousand American troops stationed in the country. Most were young, and many were abroad for the first time. Ninety-two percent of soldiers were on unaccompanied assignments, meaning that their wives and children stayed at home.

Without the distraction of family, time on the bases, many of which were remote outposts near the North Korean border, went slowly for these young men. On weekends, thousands of them flooded Seoul. Nearly everyone ended up in Itaewon, where the things they missed, familiar food, beer and sex, were plentiful. They mobbed Hooker Hill, an alley lined with "juicy bars," male-only drinking establishments that are notorious fronts for prostitution.

The Korean police and American military police that patrolled the area were used to all sorts of bad behavior on weekends, from drug dealing to bar fights to rape. But murder, especially of a foreigner, was rare.

At the Yongsan Police Station, detectives separated the students and, assisted by interpreters, began taking their statements. Start from when you got to Seoul, they told the students.

The six had arrived at Seoul's main train station on Friday as it was getting dark. They went to a tourist booth in the train station for help finding a place to stay. The employee noted their jeans, flannel shirts and backpacks and recommended Itaewon. She phoned ahead to the Kum Sung and told the manager to hold a few rooms.

The students took the subway to Itaewon and quickly located the Kum Sung, just down the street from a Burger King and Hooker Hill. They were surprised to find that it was more flophouse than motel. The seventeen rooms were crammed into a narrow three-story building. They were barely large enough for a double bed and nightstand, and they were frequently rented by the hour.

The students giggled over the condom machines bolted to the walls and the red lights illuminating the rooms. But the married couple who ran the place quoted them an attractive rate—about $15 each for the night.

They rented three rooms on the first floor. The only couple on the trip, Finns Kati Peltomaa, twenty-one, and Tuomas Heikkinen, twenty-two, took Room 102. Jamie and Anneloes, twenty-three, took Room 103. And Kenzi and Jeroen Kuilman, a twenty-two-year-old male student from Holland, took Room 104. The sleeping arrangements in the rooms were not ideal. One person had to crawl over the other to get in and out of the bed, but it was only for two nights. And besides, they told one another, it wasn't like they had come all the way to Seoul to hang out in their motel.

That Friday night they explored Itaewon. They ate enchiladas at an American-style restaurant and visited a few bars crowded with GIs. They bought beer and stayed up late playing cards in the motel and talking. Late into the night, the Kum Sung was a busy, noisy place. Guests came and went, slamming doors and talking loudly. Around midnight, someone knocked on the door of Room 104. Kuilman, who was having trouble sleeping amid the hubbub, opened the door to an African man, who quickly apologized and said he had the wrong room. The exchange student closed the door and returned to bed.

They woke early the next day, toured the sprawling Namdaemun market, and then met their Russian classmate, Elvira Makhmoutova, twenty-five, at the train station. They spent the afternoon taking in tourist attractions, including the Seoul Tower and a traditional folk village.

After a brief stop at the motel, where Elvira rented Room 101, the students walked to an Indian restaurant for dinner. Afterward Kati said she wasn't feeling well, and she and her boyfriend, Tuomas, returned to the motel.

The five who remained walked through Hooker Hill. They had known one another only two weeks, but their friendships were growing fast. Everyone was upbeat, especially Jamie. She teased Jeroen, the lone male, about the prostitutes standing in the bar doors. In an Elmer Fudd voice, she said, "We must be very quiet. We are hunting hookers."

Kenzi reminded everyone that it was St. Patrick's Day and suggested that they should find some green beer. As the words left her mouth, the group saw a sign for Nickleby's Pub. "Green beer tonight!" it read with an arrow pointing up.

Like most bars in Itaewon on a Saturday night, Nickleby's was crowded with servicemen. Many of the GIs were members of a military running group known as a hash club and were celebrating that day's run with pitcher after pitcher of beer.

The runners were friendly and talkative and kept

the students' glasses filled with beer. Soon, Jamie, Kenzi and Anneloes were dancing with the runners. As the evening grew late, Anneloes started to feel ill, and Elvira and Jeroen became bored. It was an American scene, and a drunken one at that. The Europeans decided to head home, but the American girls were still on the dance floor and wanted to stay. We're going to stay, Jamie and Kenzi told them. The other students reminded them to be up by 8:30 the next morning to leave for a tour of the Korean War Memorial. Then they left.

Anneloes told the Korean police that she stopped on the way back from the bar to phone her boyfriend in Holland and then headed to the motel. She said she talked briefly to the manager's wife, who was sitting at the front desk. She asked for water, and the old woman waved her off.

She keyed into Room 103 and then twisted the lock on the doorknob to the open position so Jamie would be able to get in later. She said she glanced at the clock as she crawled into bed. She said she was certain it said 2, because she remembered thinking she would get six hours of sleep.

The Korean police detectives had expected Anneloes to know exactly what happened to Jamie, and they were very skeptical of her account. The body was only two feet from your head, they told her through the interpreter. How could you not hear anything?

She told them that she was a very heavy sleeper, especially when she was tired.

I don't know anything, she said.

In another interview room down the hall, Kenzi was describing how she and Jamie had remained at the bar dancing, drinking and flirting with the military men. One GI kissed and propositioned her, she said, and Jamie kissed another soldier and gave him her phone number in Daegu. But when the GIs moved on to a nightclub, she and Jamie decided to call it a night. Kenzi told investigators that she wasn't wearing a watch, but thought they had left the bar between 2 and 3:30 A.M.

Jamie was drunk enough to need help walking, and when they finally reached the motel she wanted to take a shower to sober up before bed, Kenzi said. Kenzi helped Jamie into her room and steadied her while she turned on the shower and began to undress. Kenzi said she then retired to her own room, but returned to check on Jamie once more. Finding her okay, she turned in.

Elvira and Tuomas told the police they hadn't heard anything out of the ordinary. Jeroen said he only heard Kenzi coming into their room. But Kati told the detective that she thought she might have heard the murder. Her bed in Room 102 was pushed up against the wall of Room 103.

She was awakened at about 4 A.M. by a man speaking in "an angry American accent." She remembered his words exactly: "But you are here now."

Those words were followed by a noise that was hard to describe, she said. It was a low groan or soft scream—"almost like when an individual is getting hurt by somebody else." That, she said, was followed by a stomping, which continued on and off for three to five minutes.

She then heard a male voice say, "Let's go," followed by at least two sets of footsteps in the hall. Moments later, she heard a woman moaning weakly, accompanied by five to ten taps on the wall.

"I would hear a tap and then a moan," she told the police. She said she was so scared that she woke up her boyfriend, Tuomas, but he urged her to go back to sleep.

She broke into tears.

"I didn't know it was Jamie at that time and I was afraid, so I didn't go out," she said ruefully.

CHAPTER 2

THE FIRST CAUCASIAN

The husband and wife who ran the Kum Sung Motel had no illusions about their clientele. Mainly foreigners, the guests were generally seeking a cheap place for prostitution, drug use or other illicit activities. In fact, when the panicked exchange students dragged the motel manager to Room 103 that morning, he glanced at the dead body, shrugged and said one of the few words he knew in English: "Hooker."

As the police officers and detectives swarmed the Kum Sung, the husband, Chae-Kwang Sin, shooed his wife into the couple's tiny apartment and then watched from the entrance as his customers were turned out of their rooms and questioned. Like every weekend night, the motel was booked full.

The lobby, if it could be called that, was a dim hallway that ran about fifteen feet from the front door to a low counter with a sliding Plexiglas window that looked in on the couple's apartment. The counter was only about two feet off the floor so that Sin and his wife, Chong-Sun Pak, could rent rooms in the middle of the night without rising from their sleeping mats.

For eleven years, the couple had managed the motel for an elderly uncle, and as Sin watched the officers string up crime scene tape, he wondered how the murder would affect business. The work was tough enough already. Sin and Pak, both in their early fifties, were the sole employees, responsible for cleaning the rooms, laundering the sheets, emptying the trash and keeping the books. No matter the day, month, year or hour, one of them always had to be behind the little window, waiting for customers.

When detectives told Sin that he and his wife had to come down to the station for questioning, he protested. He had some information they might find interesting, he told them, but there was no reason to make his wife come. She was "feeble-minded" and hadn't seen anything anyhow, he said.

At a police substation around the corner, Sin made a startling statement: He might have seen the killer. He told detectives that sometime between 3 and 3:30 A.M., he was sitting behind the window watching karaoke videos when he heard a noise in the hall. He looked out through the window and saw a man with blood on his pants leaving the motel.

"He was a Caucasian male about 170 centimeters [five feet, seven inches] tall, a little chubby, [and] wearing a dark jacket and beige trousers," he told them. The blood was on the right side of his trouser legs.

Did you recognize him? the detectives asked. Was he one of the motel guests?

Sin shrugged. I only saw him from the back, he said.

While the detectives were questioning Sin and the exchange students, other officers remained behind to collect evidence in Room 103. In a major city in the United States, that examination would have undoubtedly meant a specialized crime scene unit with a forensic photographer, a latent fingerprint examiner, and trace evidence technicians trained to look for semen, blood, saliva, hair and fibers. Such teams would have been schooled in preventing contamination and likely worn gloves, special booties and even hairnets.

There was no such crime scene unit at the Kum Sung that morning. Korea does not have the same demand for complex forensics as the United States. Murder is rare. Seoul, with its approximately 10 million residents, had 163 homicides in 2001, the year Jamie Penich was killed. Metropolitan Los Angeles, which has a population of similar size, recorded 1,074 homicides that year.

When murder does occur in Korea, the perpetrator usually confesses. Experts put the confession rate as high as 90 percent. The very low crime rate coupled with the very high confession rate make complex forensics a luxury rather than a necessity.

The men gathering up the clothing, hairs and other evidence were not scientists, but rank-and-file officers. In Korea, trained technicians generally stay in the lab, and at the time of Jamie's murder, they did not teach police officers proper collection and preservation of evidence.

From the start, there were problems with the way things were done at the Kum Sung crime scene. In an effort to establish Jamie's identity, the young patrolmen who first arrived moved the black fleece jacket from her face and turned her over to look for the tattoo in the middle of her back. They did this before taking photos or making sketches. They tossed bloody clothes and sheets into a pile on the bed.

The patrolmen also allowed a mortuary technician to walk around the room and approach the body before detectives took over. In statements to a Seoul television station, the man admitted that he stepped in Jamie's blood and then left bloody footprints around and under the body. The same television station reported that the investigators forgot their cameras when they came to the crime scene and had to borrow a disposable camera from the mortuary technician. They also dumped multiple items of evidence into a single bag, setting up the possibility of contamination.

In addition, they were unable to lift a single fingerprint from Room 103.

Whatever their bungling, it was these officers' observations, notes and photos that became the official record of the crime scene. Room 103 was about eleven feet long and eight feet wide. Jamie's body was lying four feet inside the room, parallel to the bed. Her head, arms and torso rested in the main part of the room and her legs stretched onto the vinyl flooring outside the bathroom.

Jamie and Anneloes had unpacked by dumping their

backpacks out on the floor, and their belongings—clothing, shoes, books and toiletries—were splattered with blood. The force of the attack had knocked one of Jamie's teeth across the room. There was a bloody rag near her body and a distinctive, semicircular blood-stain low on the bedroom wall near her right hand. In the bathroom, police found the clothing Jamie had worn in the bar. Nearby in the bathtub, there was a small plastic bag.

An officer inspecting the Kum Sung's lobby noticed a smudge of blood on the door handle leading out of the motel. He swabbed up the stain for lab testing.

It was difficult for the untrained officers to tell much from Jamie's bruised and bloody body, but as they leaned over her, two things drew their attention. First, in the middle of her chest there was a small pool of saliva. It appeared someone spat on her as she lay on the floor.

The second thing they noticed was perhaps the most compelling piece of evidence at the crime scene. On her right cheek and chest they saw strange patterns. Looking closer, they saw the marks were footprints made by heavy military-style boots. She had been stomped to death, they realized. They had noticed a single bloody footprint with heavy treads in the foyer. Was this from the mortuary assistant or the killer? The officers did not know, but a quick-thinking officer found a piece of white printer paper and placed it over the print to make a permanent impression.

In the United States, large law enforcement laboratories have technicians who specialize in footprint analysis, but the Korean police did not. Instead, they dispatched a few patrolmen to the shoe stores on Itae-won's main street. Their instructions were to determine the print's shoe size and brand.

The patrolmen arrived back at the police station with a dozen boots. They told the detectives that the print was a men's size 9½ and that the tread was fairly common, matching several styles of boots made by Skechers and Timberland.

Back at the police station on the morning of the eighteenth, the investigators huddled and listed their evidence so far: A pretty young victim who had been partying with GIs is killed and left in the nude. An earwitness hears an American accent. An eyewitness sees a Caucasian fleeing. Military-style boots are the murder weapon.

The Korean detectives looked at one another and nodded. It was time to get the Americans involved. Under an arrangement known as the Status of Forces Agreement, Korean police can request the U.S. Army's help in investigating a felony outside a base if American personnel are involved. By lunchtime, agents from the army's Criminal Investigation Command had arrived at the Yongsan Police Station and were conducting interviews.

That afternoon, police loaded Jamie's body into a van and drove across the Han River to the National Institute for Scientific Investigation. NISI is Korea's government-run morgue and forensic laboratory, and its pathologists perform the autopsies in virtually every murder, suicide and fatal accident in the country. Despite its important function and impressive name, the agency's headquarters is a squat, unassuming building on a side street of a lower-class neighborhood. The entrance to the morgue is lined with crushed Daewoos and burned-out Hyundais from the traffic wrecks that are NISI's most consistent source of work.

The request for the autopsy didn't come from the police who brought Jamie's body to NISI, but from a prosecutor. In Korea, where every part of society is highly stratified, police are considered blue collar and uneducated. They must go through prosecutors, white collar and very learned, to request an autopsy from pathologists, who are of a similar education level and professional class. This difference is emphasized even in the layout of the morgue's examining rooms. A bright yellow line bisects the floor about ten feet from the body, and police are not permitted to cross the line at any time.

Jamie's autopsy was assigned to a pathologist named Kyong-Mu Yang. Not only would detectives from the Korean National Police witness the autopsy, but because the victim was American and the suspects GIs, his boss, the lab director, and representatives of the Army would also be present.

Five years later, Yang can point to the exact spot in the morgue where he stood as he unzipped the body bag.

"It was the first Caucasian I had ever examined, so I remember it well," said Yang, a tall, soft-spoken man.

At the time, Yang was thirty-four and had conducted six hundred autopsies, but the American's murder took him aback.

What cruelty, he thought as he stared down at Jamie's disfigured face.

As he examined her, Yang called out his findings to the witnesses. Some object, apparently a boot, had struck her face, neck and chest repeatedly and forcefully, causing bruising, cuts and abrasions. The blows had rained down particularly hard on the left eye socket, which was severely damaged, and the right ear, which was almost severed. There were partial tread marks in that area as well as on her left shoulder. The impact had fractured her jaw in two places and broken one of her molars in half.

Yang noted three linear bruises, like stripes, crossing her right jaw line. They were just millimeters apart, and they were distinct from the damage caused by the boot. He also observed a long, oval-shaped bruise stretching across her back from one armpit to another. It also did not appear to be caused by the boot. There were several bloody fingerprints on her calves as if the killer had spread Jamie's legs or perhaps dragged her by her calves.

Yang swabbed the drop of saliva between her breasts for further testing. Jamie's mouth was bloody, but the saliva was clear, which investigators thought was a strong indication that the spit was from the attacker and not the victim.

The fact that she had been found naked led Yang to look for signs of sexual assault. But while the upper part of her body was savaged, the lower part seemed untouched. There were no bruises or other sign of trauma around her genitals or on her thighs. The police at the scene had swabbed the outside of her genitals for semen or DNA and sent the swabs to the NISI laboratory. Yang performed a more extensive rape kit and sent the material to the lab for analysis.

Her hands were free of cuts and torn fingernails, indicating Jamie had not tried to defend herself.

Yang listed the cause of Jamie's death as strangulation, defined as any deprivation of oxygen. The doctor said he believed she died when a boot blow crushed her windpipe or in the minutes after, when blood hemorrhaging from the mouth and neck obstructed the flow of air. Considering Kati Peltomaa's account of moaning and tapping on the wall after the assault, the second cause of death seemed more likely. Based on her body temperature, he put the time of Jamie's death at 3 A.M. with a margin of error of 2.8 hours, meaning that she had died sometime between midnight and 6 A.M.

Before the autopsy, the detectives had given Yang a photocopy of the shoeprint like the one they had lifted from the motel room floor. They were not sure whether the print was the killer's or their clumsy mortuary assistant's, and they asked Yang to try to match it to the tread marks on Jamie's face and chest. The investigators stood at the yellow line as Yang leaned close to the tread marks.

The problem, he told them, was that the marks were only partial prints: a few sections of tread here, a few others there. It also appeared that the killer's foot had slipped slightly each time it made contact with Jamie's smooth skin, skewing the pattern. Yang could not solve the boot print problem created by sloppy crime scene preservation.

All I can say is that it is a similar boot in pattern and tread width, he told them.

As he finished the autopsy, Yang began packing up

samples of her blood and hair for lab testing. The witnesses drifted away, and Yang was alone with Jamie's
body. He had gone into pathology a decade before as a
way to avoid mandatory military, but he had come to
like the work and saw in it a reverence for humanity.

"To me, they are dead people without spirits, but they
are not specimens," he explained.

Yang and his wife had recently had their first child, a
daughter, and he found himself wondering what sort of
man would do this to a woman and what sort of woman
would end up in this position. He looked at the tattoo on
her back, a map of the world with the United States at
the center, and shook his head. In Korea, women from
nice families did not get tattoos.

*Maybe she's not from a good background. Maybe
she doesn't have much education. Maybe that's why
she got this tattoo*, he thought.

Four hours south of Seoul, a car carrying Keimyung
University's director of international affairs sped along
a highway. Inside, the director, Dr. Hye-Soon Kim, fran-
tically punched numbers into her cell phone. "Are there
any foreign students at your station, officer? No? Have
you heard of students at any other station?"

Dr. Kim, a sociologist who was new to the director's
job, had been at an office retreat on the coast when one
of her staffers received the strange phone call. It was
clearly one of their students, but they could make out
only a few words, including "murder" and "Seoul," before a Korean man began shouting in the background
and the call clicked off. Now Dr. Kim and her staff

were phoning every police station in the capital as they rushed back to the university.

By the time they pulled through Keimyung's gates, they knew that Jamie Penich was dead and the other students were being questioned by Korean police. Dr. Kim tracked down the university president at the campus chapel, where he was attending Sunday services, and briefed him on what had occurred in Itaewon. In the fifty-year history of the very conservative school, Dr. Kim was the only woman to hold a high administrative position at the school. Her academic work focused on outsiders in dominant cultures, including women in Korea's male-dominated society, and she was always very cognizant of her own position at the university.

The president told her that she should handle the incident, whatever it turned out to be.

"I think I should go to Seoul," she told him.

Do what you think is best, he replied.

As Dr. Kim walked away, she realized that with the time difference it was Saturday night in the United States. She did not know the names of anyone at the University of Pittsburgh, let alone their home numbers. It would be thirty-six hours before any of them were in their offices. By then, the story would be on the wire services.

I have to call Jamie's parents, she thought.

Five years later, in a campus coffee bar, Dr. Kim sighs as she recalls that moment.

"I was the one who had to deal with it," she says, shaking her head and looking out across the chairs and tables where Jamie and the other exchange students once sat. Dr. Kim's short, spiky hair and funky glasses would be fairly standard in the women's studies department of an American university, but at conservative Keimyung, they seem to be a conspicuous declaration of difference from the mainstream.

She says that after speaking to the president, she went to her apartment near campus to make the call. Her husband and two daughters were there. She looked at the girls, who were then in elementary school, and began to shake.

I can't do it, she thought.

She turned to her husband and said, "Give me a scotch on the rocks in the biggest cup we have."

He handed her the drink, and she downed it. Then she picked up the phone. For decades, she had dissected gender stereotypes and their cultural meaning, but as she waited for the international call to go through, she found herself clinging to a very Korean idea.

If you tell the man, she said to herself, *he will be stronger and less emotional.*

Patty Penich knew there was something wrong before the second ring. No one ever called their house in the middle of the night. She rolled over in bed and lifted the receiver.

"Hello?"

There was the echo of an international connection, and then a woman with an accent said, "May I speak to Mr. Penich?"

The question was like a blow. She sat up in bed.

"Who is this? Is something wrong?" she stammered.

The woman paused and then repeated herself.

"May I speak to Mr. Penich?"

Patty called out for her husband to pick up the extension.

"This is Brian Penich," he said.

Dr. Kim identified herself.

"I am sorry," she said. "Jamie's dead."

For a second, there was silence, and then the screaming started.

CHAPTER 3

SHE HAD SEEN THE WORLD

Years afterward, even talking about the horrible midnight call from Korea levels Brian and Patty Penich. Sitting in the living room of the small, meticulously kept home that he built, Brian stares down at the coffee table and recalls Dr. Kim's words.

"'Jamie's dead. Jamie's murdered. Jamie's been strangled,'" he quotes softly. Tears slide down his face and, embarrassed, he attempts a half smile. A factory maintenance worker, he is a tall, athletic-looking man with enormous hands and few words.

"I think the woman was very upset herself. She didn't really know what to say," he says.

Sitting in a chair on the other side of the room, Patty says nothing, but she clenches her jaw and looks away from a graduation photograph of Jamie on the dining room table. It shows a young woman who is a mirror of her mother, petite with chestnut hair and bright, almost mischievous eyes.

The Penichs raised Jamie and her two sisters in Derry, a community of three thousand in a picturesque part of Pennsylvania coal country known as the Laurel Highlands. The town is about an hour and a half east of Pittsburgh, but it seems even more remote.

Derry sits at the bottom of a small valley surrounded by lavender ridges. Ninety-nine percent of the town is white, and one in ten residents has a college degree. The average household income is just below $30,000. It is too small for a Wal-Mart or a movie theater or even a McDonald's. The downtown consists of the post office, a dollar store, a pharmacy and a small grocery catering mostly to seniors who don't want to drive out to the supermarket on the highway.

For much of the twentieth century, Derry was a bustling place. Immigrants came from Italy and Eastern Europe to mine the Highlands for coal, and their children and grandchildren found work in local factories like Westinghouse and at the railroad wheelhouse in the center of town. But in the 1970s and 1980s, the steel industry collapsed. Westinghouse closed, the wheelhouse was torn down and jobs were difficult to find.

Some people saw a dying town and left for better opportunities, but a core group stayed, and the experience of terrible economic times seemed to intensify their feelings for Derry.

Maybe Derry didn't have mansions or museums, but it had the mountains and the lake and nice people you had known your whole life.

"It's still the most beautiful place in the world," explained Karen Keirin, a high school music teacher who grew up in Derry. "The mines are gone, the mill closed, but it's still beautiful."

The shrinking of the town made an insular place even more close-knit. Jamie's parents are typical of Derry. They grew up a mile apart and began dating in 1974 when Patty was in high school and Brian had just started a job at the factory where he still works. They were married when Patty graduated.

Jamie was born in 1979, a year after her sister Jennell and two years before her sister Amanda. The three were close, and one of the few photos of Jamie's childhood the Penichs can bear to display shows the three little girls giggling and holding one another.

From an early age, however, Jamie was different. She loved new experiences the way other children loved their favorite blanket.

"This is a girl who walked into kindergarten the first day and said, 'Go home, Mom,'" Patty recalled.

The nun who taught her parochial school class that year, Sister Nunziatina, was from an Italian missionary order, and she spoke to the children in Italian, French and broken English. They were captivated.

"They just loved her. She would dance and sing to them in three languages and they would follow her around like she was the Pied Piper," Suzanne Markiewicz, the mother of a classmate, remembered.

Whether because of Sister Nunziatina or some other force, Jamie became obsessed with maps and traveling. She watched travel shows like other kids watched *Teenage Mutant Ninja Turtles*. She collected maps and globes. Each Christmas, she asked for a subscription to *National Geographic,* and she would sit quietly for hours poring over the map inserts: the topography of Russia, Africa by tribe, bird species on the Galapagos. It didn't matter where or what so long as it was far from Derry.

"She had a wanderlust. She didn't want to be just here. She wanted to see what was out there too," said her mother.

For Brian and Patty, a homemaker, their daughter's ambition was astonishing. They had lived their entire lives in a place where diversity meant some people were Catholics and others Presbyterians, and where a long trip was the drive to Pittsburgh. But their young daughter was talking about traveling around the world.

In Derry, the pinnacle of a young woman's life is the high school prom. The actual dance is no different than that at any other school: big dresses, big hair and limousines. What sets Derry apart is the Grand March. On the afternoon of the dance, a thousand people pack the auditorium to see each couple strut across an elaborately decorated stage as their names are announced. Almost everyone in Derry seems to want to attend, and to comply with fire codes, the school makes special tickets.

"We add extra chairs, and we still have people standing," Diane Mogle, the guidance counselor who runs the prom, said. "At least another 1,000 people would come if they could get tickets. I used to tell people we could fill Three Rivers Stadium if we knew the weather was going to be nice."

For many students, that slow walk across the stage to the cheers of family and neighbors is the most treasured memory of their youth.

Jamie skipped her prom. And graduation too.

At Derry Area High School, Jamie had a large group of friends who hung in the middle ground between the popular kids and the geeks. Jamie wanted to try everything. Although she was just five feet, two inches tall and 110 pounds, she loved sports. She played tennis. She swam. She was on the debate team and helped out with the Special Olympics. She was on the tennis and swim teams, played saxophone in the marching band and participated in forensics and international cultures club.

She had grown into a quiet but confident teenager. She rarely raised her hand, but she always knew the answer. Everyone close to her well knew that she was not long for Derry.

"She was always very quiet, but somehow behind that there was a very clear desire of a young girl who was not going to be defined by a small town all her life," her English teacher, Linda Warner, remembered.

In Derry, the teachers were often the most educated and cosmopolitan citizens. They frequently lectured their students to think outside the borders of what some jokingly termed "May-derry."

"An idea dies in the world, and ten years later, it gets to Derry," one teacher chided her students. But many of Jamie's classmates could not fathom living anywhere else.

"Some of our kids, you just know, they are going to

be here forever. Just by the way they act, who they run with, what they talk about, you can tell that they don't see that there's a great big world out there," history teacher and swim coach Jeff Kelly, said.

Kelly remembered that on the bus back from swim meets, the "Derryites" would sit in the back, talking loudly about what was going on in high school and who had set a record and where they were going to hang out that weekend.

Jamie, he said, sat in the middle with the coaches.

"We'd talk about world events and politics and a lot of different things. It was just another sign that she thought of this as small potatoes, that she was looking for something so much greater," he said.

During her junior year, she began dating a football player named Jason Young.

"I remember our first conversation on the phone was about some crisis that was going on in Russia, and she was really impressed that I knew about it," he remembered.

On dates, they would often drive by St. Martin's, the church where her parents were married and she was baptized. Even if she was in the middle of a sentence, she would stop and make the Sign of the Cross as the small red brick chapel flew by the window.

She talked to Young a lot about traveling and leaving Derry, something he found difficult to understand.

"Most of us, we never pictured ourselves gone from here, but she did," he explained. She told him she was thinking about spending her senior year as a foreign exchange student. For months, he tried to talk her out of it, but for every point he raised, she countered with a reason that she should do it. She applied to a Rotary program and got a scholarship to Belgium.

She was to leave in August. Jamie and Young broke up around that time, but they remained friends. Shortly before she was to leave, she told him she was having second thoughts.

"She was worried about being away from her parents and her grandparents. It was like the sensible side was coming out. 'I gotta stick around to go to the prom. I want my parents to see me march,'" Young remembered.

But he wouldn't hear it.

"She had done such a great job of talking me into it that I thought the right thing to do was to talk her back into it. And I did. I told her she had to go," he said.

Jamie left before school started in Derry, and she returned in June after graduation. During the year, she perfected her French and traveled throughout Europe. She got her nose pierced and the map tattoo on her back. She told her parents how she'd become lost in Venice. They were terrified, but she was laughing.

"She didn't care. It was an adventure. Everything with her was an adventure," Patty said.

A few years later, on her application for the Korean study-abroad program, she wrote about being a foreign exchange student.

"It is the best overall experience I have ever had doing anything," she wrote.

The summer she got back, she and Young went rock climbing on the ridge above Derry. When they got to the top, they looked down at the town.

"I said how beautiful it was and how I hadn't realized

it before. Jamie was just like, 'no it's really not that nice
around here at all. There are lots better places.' She had
seen the world," he said.

The phone call with Dr. Kim was short. The Penichs
had so many questions, but she knew little beside the
one horrible fact: Jamie was dead.

"What should we do? Should we come there?" Brian
asked. Patty, too upset to talk, was silent, but Brian's
voice was loud and beseeching.

Dr. Kim looked down at Jamie's file in front of her.
Derry, Pennsylvania. She knew some American geog-
raphy from brief teaching stints in Hawaii and Utah.
They are probably rural people, she thought.

She hesitated and asked, "Do you have a passport?"

"No," Brian said with frustration tinged with panic.
Why would they ever need passports? It was Jamie
who liked to go away. "Where do I get one? How?"
he asked.

Just wait where you are, she said. I am going to Seoul
to find out more.

In Seoul, Dr. Kim found the exchange students at
the Yongsan Police Station. Although officials from
their various embassies had been summoned to the
police station, the students seemed eager for help from
someone they knew. Dr. Kim was surprised at how
disheveled they looked with their dirty clothes, shower
shoes and cowlicked hair. Since their belongings were
locked behind police tape in the Kum Sung, she sent
assistants out to buy clothes and toiletries.

The police were still interviewing Kenzi, but Dr. Kim

gave the others a prepaid phone card, and one by one they called their parents from a pay phone in the corridor. She could not make out the words, but their crying echoed down the hall.

Dr. Kim arranged hotel rooms for the students, and eventually the police told Elvira, Jeroen, Kati and Tuomas that they could leave the station. There were still more questions for Anneloes and Kenzi, and Dr. Kim waited for them. Korean police investigators and army agents went in and out of the interview rooms.

At one point, Kenzi exited one of the rooms. She was angry about the questions and the interpreters. They were accusing her and Anneloes of having something to do with it, she told Dr. Kim. The Korean woman tried to be reassuring, but Kenzi snapped at her.

"Why is everyone else being allowed to make international calls for free and not me?" she asked.

Dr. Kim was taken aback by the young girl's tone, but she handed the card to Kenzi, who took it and walked away to phone her mother. *Of course, these questions would give anyone a short temper*, Dr. Kim thought. *They are only youngsters and they are probably being berated by these Korean officers.*

She approached a Korean detective and told him she was concerned about how her students were being treated.

"They are strangers here, and we are like ambassadors. If they have some sort of traumatic experience in Korea, it is really not good," she told him. She bowed slightly and clasped her hands together in the most supplicant pose she could think of. "Please, I'm begging you, be good to them."

The detective shook his head.

"It's not us. It's the Americans. They are very tough," he said.

As he spoke, a tall American in a uniform swept by them. Dr. Kim considered talking to him, but she was too intimidated.

She sat back down in the hall. *Please let the killer be a non-Korean*, she prayed silently.

Kenzi would later say she was relieved when American investigators arrived. The interpreters at the police station seemed to have only an elementary grasp of English. The students, who knew only a little Korean, caught them in mistranslations and noticed that the statements they typed up were awkwardly worded and rife with grammatical mistakes.

"I was under the intuition that some female was strike by a male" was how one interpreter rendered Kati's statement that she heard a woman being assaulted by a man.

With the army investigators, there was no need for translators. The Americans were from the local office of the Criminal Investigation Command, a nine hundred-agent-strong unit that functions as the army's detective bureau, investigating felonies with a connection to the service. The agents from the CID—the command is still identified by its old name, Criminal Investigation Division—were only assisting the Korean police in the investigation, but they quickly took the lead. Ten of the army's forty-five agents in Korea were assigned to the Penich case.

That afternoon, some of the agents drove Anneloes and Kenzi from the police station to their headquarters at the sprawling Yongsan Garrison, a 630-acre base in the center of the city, for additional questioning. Neither woman objected. They both said they wanted to help find Jamie's killer and would do anything to help the American agents. The CID and the military police shared a building on a rise on the north side of the base known as MP Hill.

As the Koreans had, the CID agents initially focused on Anneloes. The Kum Sung's rooms were tiny, and by her own admission, the pretty Dutch student had been an arm's length away from a very brutal murder. She had to know something, they reasoned.

Anneloes told them she woke up twice very briefly during the night. Once, someone had opened the door of Room 103. The second time, a hand was touching her shoulder. Neither alarmed her, she said, because she was expecting Jamie, and she immediately drifted back to sleep.

As far as the murder, she said, she knew nothing. The agents pressed her repeatedly on the point, but she insisted she was a very deep sleeper. The agents were skeptical. Their Korean colleagues who had questioned Anneloes shortly after the murder were convinced she was lying. Either the killer threatened you into silence or you yourself are the killer, one detective told her. They arranged for her to see a hypnotist, but after he consulted with Anneloes, the doctor told investigators she was not a good candidate. She was not in shock and did not seem to be blocking anything out. She simply was asleep when the relevant events occurred, he told them.

Frustrated with Anneloes, the army agents turned

to Kenzi, the last person known to have seen Jamie alive. In a small office on MP Hill, the agents sat down across a table from the nineteen-year-old. She was plump and five-foot-seven, with long, strawberry blond hair, freckles and bright blue eyes. The freckles and the baby fat in her face made her look younger than her age, but when the army investigators began talking to her, they discovered a mature young woman.

The CID agents wanted a complete accounting of the contact between the young women and GIs at the bar, and Kenzi proved a gold mine. In contrast to Anneloes, who had become increasingly hostile in the face of the investigators' suspicion, Kenzi seemed accommodating and respectful. She had grown up on a string of American bases and embassy compounds, and she was used to talking to military men. She also knew how to make the best of tough situations.

"Five different schools in six years and elected to student council in every one. That's Kenzi," her mother would often say.

It was that outgoing personality that had led to meeting the soldiers at Nickleby's. In the ladies' room just before midnight, she had struck up a conversation with an army wife. The woman was at the bar with the runners from the hash club. She introduced Kenzi to the hashers.

"I went and got Jamie and we started dancing. We were all dancing together," she said.

Soon, Jamie was slow-dancing with a hasher named Josh—"a smaller guy, about five-eight with a military haircut, dirty blonde hair, had a big smile."

Kenzi began dancing with Nick, another hasher. He

was manning the pitcher of green beer and kept filling up the girls' glasses, she said.

"He looked more Latino or Hawaiian, had darker hair and light olive skin, about five-ten, medium build," she told them.

Kenzi said she turned her back to get the other exchange students, and when she returned, Jamie and Josh were making out on the dance floor. The European students were tired and bored and at 2 A.M., they left.

Jamie pulled Kenzi aside and told her that she'd given Josh her number at the university. Was it possible she told him where she was staying in Seoul? the investigators asked.

"I don't know," Kenzi told them. "It wasn't something that she would do."

Kenzi said that while dancing with Nick, she bumped into a tall, well-built soldier named Vincent. He was more muscular than the hashers and didn't seem to know them. The two sat down in a booth away from the dance floor and began chatting. Kenzi said she mentioned she wanted to visit Jeju Island, a tropical resort off Korea's southern coast. He said he was planning a trip there. "If you come home with me tonight," she quoted him as saying, "I'll cover all your expenses."

"I told him no, but he was insistent. Finally, I told him I had to go, and then I went back on the dance floor," she said.

About 3 A.M., Kenzi continued, Nick told them that the hashers were moving on to Stompers, a nightclub on Hooker Hill. He invited them along, but

Jamie and Kenzi told him they had to be up early for sightseeing.

She said that although she hadn't looked at her watch, she thought they left Nickleby's about 3:15 A.M.

"Jamie had a lot to drink, and I was helping her walk," she told them. Somehow, they got turned around and ended up near Hooker Hill. Kenzi said she realized where she was and turned down an alley toward the Kum Sung.

As they turned, she said, she saw Vincent and another man walking in the opposite direction. She and Vincent acknowledged each other with a wave, she said, and then the women headed for the hotel.

"I didn't look back to see if he was following us, but I didn't hear anything," she told them.

She said that as they walked to the motel, Jamie began talking about taking a shower. She was convinced it would help her sober up. Kenzi said she helped Jamie to her room. Anneloes was asleep so the two women quietly went into the bathroom. Kenzi said she had turned on the water while Jamie undressed. She left as Jamie was getting into the shower.

She went to her room and climbed over Jeroen into bed. After two or three minutes, she decided to go check on Jamie.

"I went to her room, knocked on the door and asked her if she was okay and she replied, 'yes,'" Kenzi told them. She said she hadn't checked the door to see if it was locked, but that there was no one in the hall and no unusual sounds from inside the room. She returned to her bed and fell asleep.

She told the agents that she remembered some of

the hashers had cameras in the bar and were taking pictures of her, Jamie and one another.

The CID agents were thrilled with the level of detail Kenzi had provided about the soldiers. While she sat in the small office, they began tracking down the GIs.

CHAPTER 4

THE HASHERS

"Did you have sex with Jamie?"

"No, I did not."

"Did you go to the hotel where Jamie and her friends were staying?"

"No, I did not."

"Did you kill Jamie?"

In a small office on MP Hill, Sergeant Joshua Harlan stared across a desk at two CID agents and shook his head.

"No," he replied.

By sunset on the day Jamie was murdered, army investigators had begun to identify the soldiers with whom she spent her final hours. Based on the boot prints and the interviews with Kenzi, Kati and the motel owner, the investigators felt they had a fairly good handle on what had happened: A GI met Jamie in Nickleby's and then went to her motel room with a friend expecting a liaison. Denied, he became violent and killed her. It was just a matter of locating the men Kenzi had seen talking to Jamie and determining which one was the killer.

From Kenzi, they knew most of the men were in a running club. A call to the bar established the group was the Yongsan Kimchi Hash House Harriers. Hash clubs exist in cities around the world, and their motto is "a drinking club with a running problem." The emphasis is fun and socializing rather than athleticism, and runs often include beer, Jell-O shots and practical jokes. Every member has a nickname, most with a sexual connotation. There were about seventy members of the Yongsan group, and the vast majority was American military.

Famed for their partying, the hashers were welcome regulars at Nickleby's and Stompers. At Stompers, they had made friends with the bartenders and frequently commandeered a security camera to shoot video of themselves dancing, drinking and making out. The club even showed some of the video from past weekends' revelries on screens near the dance floor. The CID got the tapes and showed them to Kenzi. She sat in front of the screen pointing out the men she recognized from Nickleby's.

By that Sunday afternoon, army investigators were on the phone with one of the hash club's leaders, Natalie Langley.

"There's been a murder," an army investigator explained. "We need the full names of everyone in Nickleby's last night."

The first located was Harlan, a twenty-four-year-old from Great Falls, Montana, who worked at the base hospital as a repairman for dental equipment. Outgoing and handsome, Harlan was nicknamed "Kiwi Kandy" by some female hashers from New Zealand who, after a few beers, often tried to take his shirt off.

The agents were waiting at Harlan's barracks that afternoon when he returned from a movie matinee. They placed him in handcuffs and asked for permission to search his room.

Go ahead, he said. What's this about?

The agents did not answer. He watched from a squad car as a group of them picked through his clothes. They asked his roommate what Harlan had been wearing the night before, and the soldier pointed out jeans, a black spandex shirt and black boots with lug soles. One agent scanned the room with a special light that detects blood, semen and other biological materials.

When they were done, they drove Harlan to headquarters and told him he was a suspect in the murder of Jamie Penich.

The CID officers told him she had been found dead at the Kum Sung Motel. Harlan seemed stunned.

Yeah, I was at the bar, Harlan told them. And yeah, I talked to her, but I don't know anything about this. He said he had gone to Nickleby's with other hashers, the same as every Saturday night after their run. One of the women in the group introduced him to Jamie, and they slow-danced for two songs.

"While we were dancing, she kissed me about two times," he told them.

Harlan said Jamie was nice, but too drunk for his taste.

The way "she kissed me and the way she was dancing, she was not really stable," he told them.

He took her phone number, but wasn't interested, he said. He quickly moved on to another young woman. She was a tall, striking British brunette named Nicki who said she was an exotic dancer in the casino show at the Sheraton. As they talked, he lost track of Jamie. He and Nicki left the bar around 2 A.M. to go to the nightclub Stompers, and just before sunrise, they went back to her room at the Sheraton.

"I was there until one this afternoon," he told them.

The CID agents told Harlan they found his story hard to believe. You have Jamie, this drunk girl who obviously likes you, and you don't try to take her home? Do you really expect us to believe that? they asked.

Five years later, Harlan can still remember his response.

"I told them, 'Look, this girl was drunk and getting more intoxicated all the time. I have two little sisters, and when I'm out cruising for chicks, I think about them. I would never want someone to take advantage of them,'" he recalls.

"The CID guys were like, 'Wow, a soldier with morals. That's a rarity,'" he says.

The agents told Harlan to make a list of the names and numbers of everyone who could vouch for his story, starting with Nicki. While they were talking in the office, another CID agent called in from the hall.

I've got his boots here and they don't match, the man shouted.

"I looked at them and said, 'Sounds like good news to me,'" Harlan recalls.

Still, the agents took him to the base hospital, where

he voluntarily gave samples of his hair as well a cheek swab for genetic testing. A technician also took scrapings from under his nails for DNA testing and searched his body for bruises or scratches.

When they dropped him back at his barracks, the sun was coming up. The interview had gone all night.

Kenzi Snider was on MP Hill late that Sunday night. She was looking at photos of soldiers, trying to match the formal poses to laughing, drunken faces from Nickleby's. Around midnight, the CID agents told her they would drive her back to her hotel. As they walked into the parking lot of their headquarters, they encountered some other agents and a suspect. It was Nick, the olive-skinned GI from Nickleby's. The agents began talking, leaving Nick and Kenzi standing together a few feet apart.

Nick stared down at the ground with his hands in his pockets.

"I'm sorry about your friend," he said.

She nodded. It was an awkward moment.

Nicholas Baer, a twenty-eight-year-old staff sergeant from South Carolina, was trained as an ophthalmologist's assistant and worked at the eye clinic in the base hospital. In the hash club, he was known as "Pound Cake," a reference to the time he'd dropped a case of beer on his crotch.

As with Harlan, the CID agents had searched Baer's barracks before bringing him in for questioning. He had handed over the clothes he had worn to the bar: tan pants, a green shirt and Skechers boots.

When they asked him about what he had done the night before, he told them that his Saturday night followed the pattern of most of his Saturday nights in Korea. He hung out with the hashers, first at Nickleby's, then at Stompers. He drank and he tried to pick up women.

He said he had danced with Anneloes and Kenzi, but he barely remembered Jamie.

"I talked to her a little, but not much. She was dancing and talking with someone else," he said.

He remembered Kenzi being pulled into a booth by a muscular soldier who was not in the hash club. That must be the one named Vincent, the agents thought. Around 12:30 or 1, he and the other hashers left Nickleby's and headed to Stompers. He remained in the club until 6 A.M., he told them.

"The sun was already coming up," he said.

Who can vouch for that? the agents asked.

Baer shrugged. The club was a wild scene, crowded, loud and hot. It was easy to get separated from people. Another hasher had been with him until 4, but then that soldier went home. Baer said he had wandered through the club looking for people he knew. He talked to a woman who said she was in the air force, and he met a Korean man, but he had no idea how to contact them.

"Is there anyone you know by name that can say where you were between 4 A.M. and 6 A.M.?" an agent asked him.

"No," he acknowledged.

The CID agents released Baer that morning but

picked him up again later in the day and questioned him again. He told them he had talked to some other hashers and felt he had gone to Stompers closer to 1 A.M. He still did not have an alibi, however.

It took longer for the army to locate the third soldier Kenzi had mentioned, Vincent. He was not a member of the hash and did not live on the main Yongsan base. The CID agents were especially eager to talk to him because of Kenzi's description of his aggressive behavior in the bar, an account that Nick backed up. Maybe Vincent had gone to the Kum Sung looking for Kenzi and ended up in Jamie's room instead.

The agents pored over databases and told Kenzi that more than one hundred GIs stationed in Korea had that first name.

Kenzi looked through photos, and by Tuesday morning, a group of CID agents were traveling north toward the DMZ to Camp Casey, a base so remote that soldiers qualify for hardship pay.

The soldier they went to see was a twenty-four-year-old second lieutenant in the military intelligence service from Pennsylvania.

Five years after the murder, Vincent agreed to discuss his experience through e-mail, but he asked that his last name not be used. Now a captain serving in Iraq, he says he would rather people not know about his involvement in the case.

"I was called by my battalion's executive officer. He told me that I had to go talk to the CID, but he didn't know why," he remembers. At that point, he had been in Korea seven months and he mainly knew the CID to deal with drunken brawls between soldiers.

When he sat down to the interview, the CID agents told him they were there about an assault.

"I didn't see a fight," he said, cutting them off. "But a guy should not call the CID if he loses a bar fight."

The agents quickly told him they were not there about a bar fight, but a murder.

"I was shocked," Vincent said.

He was in Seoul that night to attend a military ball, and afterward he and a friend had gone to Nickleby's, followed by Stompers. He told the agents that he remembered Kenzi, but the name Jamie didn't mean anything to him. The agents showed him a photo of Jamie.

"I may have said hello to her," he told them.

He remembered her on the dance floor with Kenzi and "another guy who was possibly Greek, Italian or Spanish. He had dark hair and was about five-foot-eight." Although he didn't know him, the description generally fit Baer.

He said he and Kenzi had talked for fifteen minutes in a booth.

"What did you talk about?" an investigator asked.

"I asked her what she was doing here in Korea, and she said she was visiting for three months," Vincent replied.

"Did you have any intimate contact with her?" the agent asked.

"All we did was kiss for two or three seconds," he answered.

He said Kenzi never told him where she was staying, and she eventually got up and left.

Around 2 A.M., he and his friend headed to Stompers and spent the rest of the evening hanging out in clubs and bars. At 5:30, they went back to their room in the base hotel. They fell asleep watching MTV, he said.

The CID asked him about encountering Kenzi and Jamie on the street, but he denied it.

I never saw her after we were in the booth together, he insisted.

While Vincent was being questioned, other agents searched his barracks and took the clothes he said he wore the night of the murder: a Notre Dame jacket, "a green t-shirt that says 'American First, Irish Always' over American and Irish flags," blue jeans and sneakers.

Harlan, Baer and Vincent were the only soldiers Kenzi knew by name, but they were hardly the only ones interviewed. From the hashers, they had confiscated rolls of film taken in the bar and used them to track down most of the two hundred people in Nickleby's that night.

On March 23, five days after Jamie's body was found, they interviewed Michael "Mick" Kolinski at Camp Red Cloud, another remote base near the North Korean border. Kolinski was a twenty-seven-year-old infantry captain from Michigan, and in the hash club, his name was "Mount Vesuvius."

He told the agents that he remembered Jamie well. They had kissed two or three times on the dance floor at Nickleby's.

"What type of kiss was it?" one agent asked him.

"It's referred to as a French kiss," Kolinski deadpanned.

He said that about 12:30 or 1 A.M. everyone started leaving Nickleby's for Stompers and he decided to go with them.

"Why didn't you stay with Jamie or get her to go with you?" one of the army investigators asked.

"It wasn't that important to me if she stayed or went with the group," he admitted.

The agents pressed him to account for his time between 1 A.M. and 6 A.M.

Kolinski hesitated. He had been extremely inebriated, and in that way, the night was no different from many he passed in Korea. He had a wife back in the States, but his rank was too low for him to bring her to Korea. The distance and their youth were unraveling their marriage, and many nights he found himself much more intoxicated than he had intended.

Five years later, divorced and serving a second tour in Iraq, he recalled Korea as a trying time.

"It was difficult for me to be away from my wife . . . and instead of doing something constructive with my time, I probably drank too much," he said.

On St. Patrick's Day, by his own count, he drank six beers at the hash in the afternoon, twelve to fifteen at Nickleby's and four more at Stompers.

"I do not recall any of the exact times, however, I will tell you as closely as I can," he said to the agents. He told them he spent a couple of hours in Stompers with the hashers, but the crowd began to bother him and at 3:30 or 4, he left and strolled around Hooker Hill, looking for people he knew.

He walked in and out of bars, ending up in a juicy bar.

"One of the girls who works in the club pulled me into a booth to sit down," he told them. But he was too drunk to make conversation with her, and after five minutes, he passed out in the booth.

"When I woke up, it was light outside," he said.

The agents zeroed in on the period between 3:30 and 4 A.M.

"Is there anyone who can confirm your whereabouts at that time?" one agent asked.

"Not really," Kolinski admitted.

He remembers the agents as intense and angry. "They did the good cop—bad cop thing on me," he says. "I thought it was funny, but I'm in the military. I'm not the kind of person who is easily intimidated."

The CID agents seemed fairly green to Kolinski, who then commanded twenty men. It's like the mid-level supervisor telling the CEO what to do, he thought.

"One guy looked like he was about 12. It was almost comical because they looked so young," he said.

Still, he said, "I tried to be as cooperative as possible because I had nothing to hide."

He handed over the clothes he had been wearing that night: a green and blue rugby shirt with the number 3 on the back, light blue jeans, and dark brown hiking boots from Target. Like the other soldiers, he also gave hair and DNA samples.

The army investigators sent the clothes and biological samples to the NISI lab and began divvying up alibi checks. With science and good police work, it shouldn't be difficult to figure out who was lying, they thought.

CHAPTER 5

DOUBLE HAPPY

In Daegu, the terrible news from Seoul raced through the tiny community of international students. The semester was only two weeks old, but students already felt deep bonds with one another, and they were devastated.

People stood in the dorm hallways sobbing and hugging one another. Jamie was a favorite of her classmates. In a larger study-abroad program with more options for socializing, her quiet wit and intense but unshowy curiosity might have been overshadowed by bolder personalities. But Keimyung was so small, the students were forced to get to know their classmates well, and people liked her.

"She was honest, saying what she thinks, straightforward," Bakary Bakayoko, a student from the Ivory Coast and the president of the foreign students association, remembered.

Over the dinner table and at their nightly bull sessions, the students talked about politics, literature and sex. They revealed their personal histories more quickly than they would have done with strangers back home. Jamie was no exception. She told the group that she had broken up with her fiancé just before leaving for the study-abroad program.

The students were filled with questions about the murder, but their classmates who had gone on the trip with Jamie remained in Seoul, and the university administrators had few details. In the absence of information, there were rumors.

"First I heard that two guys in the nightclub were fighting because of her. Then the rumors said that she kissed one of them. The other one wasn't happy and followed her and also wanted a kiss from her. She refused, then they fought and the soldier killed her," Bakayoko remembered.

There were rumors that somehow her ex-fiancé had snuck into Korea from Pittsburgh and killed her. Students also whispered about a secret online diary Jamie was supposedly keeping and a secret boyfriend who supposedly visited her dorm late at night. None of the rumors seemed believable, but talking gave students something to do besides think about Jamie's murder.

The six students returned from Seoul the next weekend. They were broken emotionally. They tried to answer their friends' questions, but often it proved too difficult.

Bakayoko asked Kenzi about the night, but "we didn't

talk long because she was very affected by the case and was crying while we were talking," he recalled.

Dr. Kim found her international students reeling. "They were in a kind of turmoil," she said. "They were not very stable."

The students wanted to organize a memorial service for Jamie, but university officials resisted. During government protests in the 1980s, some students had been killed and others committed suicide. To discourage imitators, universities adopted a policy against public memorials for students. The foreign students were outraged, and eventually Dr. Kim went to the president and got permission for a small and discreet memorial. The students placed Jamie's photo and some flowers in the lobby of her dorm.

Even with the modest memorial and offers of grief counseling, many students told Dr. Kim they were too distraught to continue. Anneloes and Jeroen were already packing up, and other students lined up outside her office to make their own plans for leaving.

"Some just said, 'I don't want to be here anymore,' but most said, 'I don't know if I can get through this,'" she recalled. She told them the choice was theirs, but that she thought it was better to deal with the pain than to run from it.

"It will haunt you," she warned.

In the end, however, some students left. The sole American to remain was Michael Greco, a University of Rhode Island student.

In Jamie's hometown, word of her death spread slowly at first. On Sunday afternoon, the Penichs told relatives, who passed the news to friends, who told friends. Jamie's swim coach, Jeff Kelly, found out at the gas station when one of his students shouted the news across a fuel pump. Others learned from Monday's *Pittsburgh Post-Gazette* or the television news. An announcement was made in the teachers' lounge of the high school, where Amanda Penich was still a student.

It was difficult for anyone in Derry to imagine that the quiet, confident girl who played saxophone in the marching band and volunteered for the Special Olympics had been murdered halfway around the world.

Everyone had so many questions. What was Jamie doing in that neighborhood? Was it some sort of bar fight? A burglary, maybe? Were there soldiers involved?

If people in Derry imagined the Penichs had answers to these questions, they were wrong. Brian Penich had called the Pitt campus police, the American embassy, the FBI in Pittsburgh and the Korean police, and he had very little to show for it. His daughter was dead and no one seemed to be able to tell him anything.

It was beyond frustrating. He looked at his wife, too distraught to talk or leave bed, and his surviving daughters, who could not stop crying. He thought about the fruitless international calls and the details of Jamie's death and the questions from the reporters, and it was all so complicated and horrible. If he could just have her back, whatever was left of his little girl, back in Derry, it would be a little better.

When the phone rang and an administrator from Pitt asked if there was anything the university could do, Brian choked out four words: "I want her home."

On the other end of the line, Annagene Yucas, the director of Pitt's study-abroad program, felt her face flush and tears well in her eyes. She had grown up in a small steel mill town very much like Derry and heard the familiar accent of rural western Pennsylvania in Brian's voice.

Thirty years ago, when she was a senior at Pitt, her father had driven her to the airport to catch a plane to a study-abroad program in France. It was the trip that would catapult her out of her little town and into a Ph.D. program and eventually a successful career in academia. She had looked back as she boarded the plane and saw her father, a mechanic and World War II veteran, with tears rolling down his face. In the phone calls with Brian Penich, she thought of her own father.

Getting Jamie's body back home proved much more complicated than Dr. Yucas could have imagined. In one of Brian's first conversations with officials in Korea, they told him that he needed to send them $8,000. Brian couldn't believe he had heard right, but Yucas soon discovered that he had.

In dozens of calls to Korea over many days, she learned that $8,000 was the cost of shipping Jamie's body back to Derry, and that she would remain in the morgue in Seoul until the amount was paid.

Dr. Yucas knew the sum was more than the Penichs could afford. She knew that Jamie, like all study-abroad participants, had an international student ID card, and included in the price of that card was repatriation insurance. It took many calls over many days to establish that no one at the university or at the Korean National Police could find the card.

At the end of every day of futile calling, there was one final number Dr. Yucas dreaded dialing. Five years later, in her office overlooking the Pitt campus, she cringed as she recalled the phone calls to Derry.

"It was the hardest thing I've ever had to do. I would have to sit there and sort of build myself up to make the call," she said. The heartbreak in Brian's voice was so clear and she had nothing good to tell him. She was trying her hardest, but there were no answers and no progress. They had lost their daughter, and she couldn't even get this small thing sorted out.

Finally, Pitt wired $8,000 to Korea.

"We told them [the Penichs] money would not be an issue for them," she said.

On March 25, a week after her murder, a United Airlines jet brought Jamie's body home to Pennsylvania.

The experience shook Dr. Yucas. She and a colleague visited a grief counselor, and she began to consider a career change. Before Jamie, the worst thing that had ever happened to a study-abroad student was a broken ankle in a bicycle accident in Munich. That girl had been in her office six weeks later, filling out an application to go back abroad. Dr. Yucas had always felt she was making the world a better place by encouraging young people to explore it, but now she wasn't so sure.

As the plane carrying Jamie's coffin touched down in Pittsburgh, scientists from NISI's forensic laboratory were examining dozens of pieces of evidence from the Kum Sung Motel. The police officers who worked the scene handed over to technicians hairs from the floor, specks of blood from the walls and from Jamie's body, cigarette butts from an ashtray in the room and clothing belonging to Anneloes and Jamie. Dr. Yang sent samples of blood and saliva from the autopsy. As the investigation went on, investigators added hair and DNA samples from the soldiers as well as the GIs' clothing and boots. All told, NISI analyzed one hundred items connected to the Penich case.

The forensic scientists who work at NISI are the best in Korea, but getting meaningful results proved an uphill battle. Without dispute, the crime scene was contaminated. In addition to the mortuary assistant who had tromped through the blood and the junior officers who had moved Jamie's body in their search for her tattoo, at least three of the exchange students—Anneloes, Jeroen and Kenzi—had been in the room with the body, and Anneloes had actually touched it.

The officers who gathered the evidence were not the type of seasoned crime scene specialists who would have worked an American case, and their lack of training showed in how they cared for Jamie's body at the motel and packaged the evidence. They wrapped her body in a sheet and moved it to another room down the hall while they collected evidence. Investigators removed the sheet in the second room, which was far from a sterile environment, and inspected her injuries and then wrapped her in the sheet again and took her to the coroner's office. It is unclear what effect this had, but the saliva the coroner later collected from her chest was too contaminated for DNA testing. Items they deemed to be related were tossed together in big bags rather than being painstakingly cataloged. Processing such a scene in the United States might have taken two days, but in Korea, it was done in hours.

Also critical was what the police did not collect, including the shoes of the exchange students. Some of

the students remember police giving them pieces of
copy paper in the stationhouse and instructing them to
draw their treads.

Even if the police were better trained, however, the
motel crime scene still would have posed a formidable
forensic challenge. With guests changing by the hour,
Room 103 was a petri dish of human biological samples, most unrelated to the crime.

Korean scientists rely heavily on blood typing of hair
and blood samples, rather than the vastly more precise
DNA testing, which is the standard in U.S. crime labs.
Not surprisingly, the results of such testing were not
very enlightening in Jamie's case. The blood in the
room was Type B, her type. Some of the hairs were
Type O, Anneloes's type. Others, including a hair found
beneath Jamie's head, were Type A.

The blood the investigators were most interested in
was the smudge on the door leading out of the Kum
Sung. The working theory was that Jamie's assailant—
perhaps the man in the bloody pants—had rushed from
the motel with her blood still dripping from his fingers.
If his sweat or blood had mixed with hers, that smudge
would contain DNA of the killer and the victim and be
the key to the case.

Since the process of blood typing destroys the sample, the scientists decided not to type this one critical
piece of forensic evidence. Instead they used the entire
swab to get a DNA profile. The results were surprising:
The DNA was not Jamie's at all. It all belonged to one
man. They compared the profile to the DNA of the
soldiers, but none of them matched.

The results were frustrating. Was it perhaps completely unrelated to the murder? With the motel's

haphazard cleaning, perhaps it had been there for weeks. It was impossible to test the smudge against the DNA of the hairs and blood in the room because those samples were consumed in the blood typing.

In an attempt to determine whether the killer had dripped any blood in the hall, army investigators sprayed luminol, a chemical that causes blood to glow, on the floor of the motel hallway. The entire floor became fluorescent, apparently a reaction to some component of the cleaning fluid used on the floor.

A toxicology screen of Jamie's blood showed no drugs and a 0.11 blood alcohol level. The legal limit to drive in the U.S. is 0.08. The finding was consistent with what Kenzi and the soldiers told investigators: Jamie was drunk and having trouble keeping her balance.

Certainly the most mysterious finding were the results of four semen tests. Dr. Young, the pathologist, had performed an extensive rape kit during the autopsy. Lab analysis of that kit showed no sign of sexual activity. But the police had done their own test at the crime scene. Detectives had leaned over the body and swabbed Jamie's genitals. Testing of that cotton swab came back "weakly positive" for semen. The lab techs got the same result on two pair of underwear, one belonging to Jamie and the other to Anneloes. It was impossible to retest the result because the entire sample had been used for the testing.

The forensic examiner, Hui Chung An, said the weak results meant that just a small amount of semen was left, an indication that the women had sexual relations two or three days before the murder, but not on the night of the murder.

When Jamie's family and friends learned the semen test results months later, they were puzzled. It made no more sense to them than the soldiers' accounts of a wild party girl. Who was this person they were describing? Not the serious, hardworking young woman Jamie had become. As far as anyone knew, Jamie had slept with only one man, and he was her fiancé at the time. She was hardly a flirt.

"I couldn't imagine her kissing a bunch of guys and giving out her phone number. She was a very friendly person, but also a little bit apprehensive of new people. If we went out and guys were flirting with her, she'd be a little weirded out. She'd say, what do you want?" her best friend from college, Mia Scott Shea, remembered.

After high school, Jamie spent a few semesters at a community college near Derry and then transferred to the University of Pittsburgh. It was a strategy that made sense to many working-class families in the area. Why spend a lot of money on introductory courses at an expensive university when you could learn the same basics for a fraction of the price close to home?

While she was attending community college and living at home, she met a young musician named Jeff Gretz. Three years older than Jamie, he was drawn to her exuberance, intelligence and ambition.

She always knew the answer to "Final Jeopardy," and in one of their first conversations, he asked what her goals were in life.

"She said, 'Well, what I want to do is save the world,'" he recalled at a memorial service for Jamie. "Right off the bat, that tells me I'm not dealing with a normal person. She was very different. She set a goal in her mind and she did it."

At Pitt, Jamie came up with a more concrete plan to help people. She would educate different peoples about one another as an anthropology professor. She would get a Ph.D. in cultural anthropology and travel the world doing research. First, however, she had to get her bachelor's degree. She hardly took the easiest route. She was a double major in anthropology and religious studies and was working toward a certificate in Asian studies and a minor in Korean. She also held down two jobs. She worked at a day care center near campus and as a hostess at a brew pub.

On her rare days off, she would go hear Gretz play in his heavy metal band. She liked to drink, but knew how to hold her liquor, her best friend, Shea, recalled.

"She definitely knew how to handle herself. She was never out of control or stumbling around," Shea said. If she got a little drunk, she would talk very enthusiastically about cultural anthropology, but that was the extent to which she lost her inhibitions.

She and Gretz eventually moved in together and became engaged. She told her mother that she wanted to get married on the Pitt campus at Heinz Chapel, a spired building dedicated to knowledge and culture, rather than a specific religion.

Jamie and her mother went wedding dress shopping on Mother's Day 2000. With Jamie's petite frame, "she looked like the doll on top of a cake," Patty recalled.

She remained serious about her studies. She was not the sort to sleep through classes or complain about papers, no matter how tired she was.

"Some nights she was working on three of them and she would get A's on every one," Gretz remembered.

Jamie felt fortunate to be studying the subjects that she loved. She described her classes to her parents and told them about the work her professors were doing. When she went to talk to her adviser, a Japan specialist named Keith Brown, she was captivated by the artifacts he brought back from his summer sabbaticals in a small town three hours north of Tokyo.

"She started talking about studying abroad herself and I thought, yes, she's on the right track," Brown recalled.

Jamie had considered going to Japan for her junior spring, but instead decided on Korea. She had taken a beginning Korean class and was even practicing the language with a Korean-speaking preschooler at the day care.

In her application to Keimyung University, she wrote, "I take school as well as work very seriously and would be honored to be given the chance to expand my knowledge of things by studying abroad . . ."

> *I would like to study abroad for many reasons. I have a passion for traveling and being immersed in other cultures . . . I learned many difficult things by studying abroad in the past, including how to handle myself in difficult situations, how to take the good with the bad and how to survive in a strange place where I did not speak the language. I plan to use those experiences and build on them if I have the chance to study abroad again.*

She wrote that she hoped to master Korean and felt she was prepared to do so:

> *I feel that one of my greatest strengths is my ability to adapt to many varied situations. I love being challenged and I enjoy experiencing new and different things. I see the chance to study abroad as a way of challenging myself, and learning more about myself as well as others. I also see study abroad as a way of learning more about what I really want to do with my life. The first time I studied abroad in high school made me realize my love of travel and language. This time, hopefully, I can learn even more about myself.*
>
> *Overall, I see study abroad as a learning experience. I feel that I would be a perfect candidate because of my motivation and love for new things and challenges. I sincerely hope that I will be given this opportunity based on the work I have done previously and the work I plan to do abroad as well in the more distant future.*

Just before Jamie left, she broke off her engagement. She had known Gretz since she was seventeen, and he was the only serious relationship she had ever had. They still loved each other very much, but Jamie wanted to be free from any ties when she went abroad.

"Everyone knew they were going to end up together, but I think she wanted to see a little bit more of the world without being tied down," Shea recalled.

Gretz remembered their breakup conversation at Jamie's memorial service.

"She taught me a few things about letting go of ties,

not necessarily because you don't have connections with things and people, but sometimes it is best for you and everyone around you," he said.

Ending the relationship was difficult, but Jamie talked about her trip to Korea in terms of fate. Shortly before she left, she told Shea that when she got there she was going to get another tattoo: the Chinese character for double happiness.

"She said she wanted to wait until she was actually double happy to get the tattoo and for her, that wouldn't be until she was abroad," Shea remembered.

The week after Jamie's murder, Shea went to a tattoo parlor in Pittsburgh and got the characters tattooed on her wrist.

CHAPTER 6

THE MAN WITH BLOODY PANTS

Two days after Jamie's body arrived, her twenty-three-year-old sister, Jennell, sat down on her computer and typed out an e-mail to Kenzi Snider.

"All I want to know is if she was having a good time in Seoul? Did she get to see any of the sights. I just want to make sure that Jamie was happy those last few days before this tragedy," Jennell wrote on March 27. She added, "I know this must be as hard for all of you as it is for me and my family."

The following afternoon, cars carrying Jamie's classmates, coworkers and university administrators left the Pitt campus for the viewing in Derry. Annagene Yucas was in one of the vehicles. She and a colleague had visited the grief counselor for a last-minute bolstering before departing for Derry.

"I knew I wanted to be there, but I just didn't know how I could face them or what I could possibly say," Dr. Yucas recalled.

The counselor told her that there was nothing she could say to comfort the Penichs. All you can do is go and show with your presence that their daughter's life meant something to you, the woman told them.

Dr. Yucas felt too shaky to drive, and so she stared out the window of the car. The majestic university buildings of Forbes Avenue gave way to the interstate, then a highway with traffic lights and finally the twisty road that led down through the hills.

It must have struck those making the fifty-mile trip just how far Jamie had come to succeed in the academic world of Pitt.

"Jamie was really a trailblazer out of Derry. She was doing extraordinary things that nobody in her family had ever done. She was a small town girl, but she was going global," Dr. Yucas said.

At the Quinlisk Funeral Home, the line of people waiting to pay their respects to the Penichs stretched out the door and down Chestnut Street. It seemed like all of Derry was there. The funeral director, a family friend, had handled hundreds of deaths, but as he helped them make the arrangements, Patty saw tears in his eyes. She and Brian sat near the coffin they had picked out. People filed by with hugs and kind words, but everything seemed a blur.

At one point, the priest from St. Martin's leaned over to them. Normally we'd stop now and say the rosary, but there's no way everyone can fit inside, he told them. We'll just say extra prayers tomorrow.

The next morning, a procession of cars stretching two miles left the funeral home and wound its way out of town and up a hill to the bluff where St. Martin's church sits overlooking the valley. Irish farmers built it 145 years ago with brick made in Derry. It is a modest structure with just twenty-eight narrow wooden pews and a simple altar. The only thing fancy about St. Martin's is a small mural in the middle of the pressed tin ceiling, which shows Martin of Tours, a Roman soldier, giving half his cloak to a beggar.

By the time the Mass began, every seat in the church and the choir loft was filled. People clustered in the foyer and spilled out the front steps.

Jason Young, Jamie's junior year boyfriend, stood across the street watching people arrive. He remembered Jamie crossing herself each time they drove by the church, and he thought about the long conversation in which he convinced her to go to Belgium. He decided not to go in.

"I thought it would be too tough to see them lay her down," he remembered.

Dr. Yucas leaned on the arm of a colleague. When she had returned to Pitt the night before, she had gone back to the grief counselor. The woman could only reiterate what she had said a dozen times before: The family just wants to know that Jamie's life meant something.

Looking back, the Penichs cannot remember much of the service.

"I know I was there, but I couldn't tell you what was said or very much about it," Patty said.

The priest tried to say some comforting things to Brian and Patty. They were sitting with their daughters in the front row of the church near the altar rail where they had been married. Above them on the right side of the altar was a large statue. From the back of the church, the statue was easily identifiable as St. Joseph with his staff in one hand and the infant Jesus in the other. But it was only from the front, where the family sat, that one could see the Christ child was himself holding something. In his small outstretched hand was a blue globe, one last map of the world for Jamie.

After the funeral, there was a lunch in the parish hall. One by one, Pitt students gingerly approached the Penichs and introduced themselves.

Brian and Patty "were numb. They didn't know who was talking to them. At one point, I remember thinking they had the deer-in-the-headlights look. They don't even know what has hit them," Jamie's swim coach, Jeff Kelly, remembered.

Later in the afternoon, close relatives and friends returned to the Penichs' house to sit with the family. There were so many sympathy cards to open. Eventually they would fill two shoe boxes. In the middle of the quiet conversations, the phone rang.

It was Kenzi Snider.

She and Brian spoke briefly. That day, he was just focused on making it from one minute to the next, and her words of condolence barely registered. She said something about Jamie enjoying the sights in Seoul and being very happy before she died. He thanked her and hung up.

When Jennell Penich checked her e-mail, she had a similar message from Kenzi.

"It's great to know Jamie was having a good time her last days in Seoul," she replied.

The day of the funeral, Kenzi boarded a plane in Korea for the United States. Of the students who decided to leave early, Kenzi was among the last to go. It had turned out to be a more difficult choice for her than the others.

There was the financial issue. Here was a semester of school paid for with scholarships and student loans, and with only three weeks of classes, she wasn't any closer to her goal of an education degree. For some students that might not have mattered, but Kenzi had no relationship with her father, and her mother was just scraping by as a teacher in an international school in Thailand. Money was no small issue.

She was also aware of being the first student from Marshall University to participate in an exchange program in Korea. She did not want to let down her school, she said later.

Perhaps most fundamentally, there was the matter of where to go if she left Korea. While other students headed back to their hometowns and childhood bedrooms to await the next semester at college, Kenzi didn't have that option. With her father's careers in the air force and State Department, Kenzi's childhood was spent in temporary housing in five countries and three states.

"There was nothing waiting for her in the U.S.," her roommate from the Kum Sung, Jeroen Kuilman, recalled.

But at the same time, the idea of staying after Jamie's death seemed unimaginable.

"Jamie wasn't there anymore. If I hadn't seen her body, I could pretend it away, but I had seen her body, and you can't pretend that away," Kenzi said later.

Before Anneloes, Jamie's Dutch roommate from the motel, and Jeroen departed, they told Kenzi she was always welcome to visit them in Holland.

The students had known one another only a brief time, but the experience of Jamie's death seemed to bond them. In an e-mail to Kuilman ten days after the murder, Kenzi wrote, "I have finally decided what I am going to do . . . I am going to be going back to the States."

She told Kuilman that she would go to Minnesota, where her parents had grown up and where her three grown brothers lived. She would then come to Holland, she wrote, for "however long I can."

She added, "I think by that time, I am going to be needing the support from you guys (whether you like it or not heheh)."

The lights in the CID offices on MP Hill burned all night. The army agents had a pool of strong military suspects and a detailed statement from each man. It was only a matter of punching holes in the killer's story. They spent every day looking for ways they could verify or debunk their accounts.

Some were obvious. Josh Harlan, the Montana hasher whom Jamie had kissed on the dance floor, had as his alibi a one-night stand. Agents tracked the young woman to the casino where she worked. She was not happy to see them, but she confirmed Harlan's story. He was with me from Nickleby's until the next afternoon, she told them.

The alibi of Vincent, the military intelligence officer who came on to Kenzi in a booth, relied heavily on another soldier, Javier Martinez. Vincent claimed he and Martinez were together from the time they left Nickleby's for Stompers until they fell asleep watching TV in a base hotel. When they located Martinez a short time later on the same northern base, he echoed Vincent's story. They were never separated for more than a couple of minutes, he said.

The agents remained suspicious. They knew from Kenzi that Vincent was sexually aggressive in the bar and that he also saw her and Jamie as they made their way back to the motel. Maybe he and Martinez had followed the young women. The fact they were together also made them promising suspects. Kati Peltomaa, the student in Room 102, said she heard the apparent assailant talking to someone else in the hall and more than one set of footsteps leaving the scene.

But Vincent and Martinez denied ever going to the motel. They produced the names of more than ten people who could vouch for them at the pub and Stompers. Video from the nightclub, Stompers, showed them there for at least some of the night, and security cameras at the base hotel confirmed their account of arriving at the hotel at dawn.

The pair also didn't match the motel manager's description of the man with bloody khaki pants. Both were wearing jeans, and Vincent was five inches too tall and much too muscular to fit the description of the fleeing man.

There was also the matter of the boots. Investigators believed the killer wore size 9½ hiking boots. Vincent could not fit his foot into anything smaller than a size 13.

Officially, the Korean National Police remained the lead agency investigating Jamie's murder. In practice, the CID agents handled the most promising leads. Their command of English made them the sensible choice to deal with the exchange students, the soldier suspects and other expats connected to the case.

Still, the Koreans aggressively worked the perimeter of the case. They might not know much about the mating habits of young Americans, but they knew how to navigate the criminal underbelly of Itaewon.

They questioned the African peddlers who resided in the Kum Sung. None of the men seemed to remember Jamie, though, and one Nigerian told the detectives his countrymen were not capable of such a crime.

Nigerians, he said, "argue, but they do not kill persons. Especially, they do not kill female persons because they think much of female persons."

Five days after the murder, a Korean detective phoned MP Hill. We found a hooker from the Kum Sung and you're going to want to hear what she has to say, the investigator told the CID agent.

Miss Yi was a Korean woman in her twenties with heavy bangs, a broad face and a passable knowledge of English. In interviews with authorities, she never admitted that she was a prostitute. When pressed for an occupation, she said she was an unemployed dropout from a college that trained workers for the tourism industry. But when she described her own activities St. Patrick's Day night, the authorities had little doubt about her occupation.

She had gone out alone at midnight in Itaewon in three-inch heels and ended up in Stompers, throwing back whiskey and Cokes with a couple soldiers. Eventually she and a civilian army employee, an engineer from a base outside Seoul, went back to the room he had rented at the Kum Sung Motel.

In an interview with the Korean detectives on March 23, 2001, she said she had noticed two things when she walked into the shabby motel. The clock on the wall said 4:20 A.M., and the motel manager, Sin, was standing in the lobby. Apparently believing the couple wanted to rent a room, he shouted at them that the motel was booked full, but her date pulled out a key for Room 213 and dangled it in front of him.

Yi said she and the civilian army employee brushed past the manager and toward the stairs that led to the second floor. As they rounded the corner, she noticed the door to Room 103 was slightly ajar, and a man was loitering outside it.

"I can't remember his face exactly," she told the police. "He was neither black, nor white. He didn't look like a Korean man either. He looked like a South Asian man."

She said that as she passed he took about two small, hesitant steps that made her think he was pacing outside Room 103.

"His height seemed to be five-seven or five-nine and [he was] slim built. He was wearing dark pants, bright colored long sleeve shirt, and his hair style was 'white collar style,' " she said, referring to a cut that was short on the sides and back and a little longer in the front.

She began climbing the stairs when she heard the motel owner yelling at the man. She couldn't make out Sin's words, but she turned and looked back down the stairs.

"The owner said something to him and [the man] grabbed the Room 103 door handle as if he was about to go in the room. I didn't see if he actually went into the room or not," she said.

She and her date repaired to Room 213, had sex and passed out. She never heard any sounds of an assault.

Yi told detectives that she wasn't sure if she would recognize the man if she saw him again. The hall was dark and she was drunk.

When the army agents heard the account, they were excited. The time was within five minutes of when Kati Peltomaa, in the room next door, heard the sounds of an assault.

Was the man in the hall waiting for an accomplice to kill Jamie? the investigators wondered.

The CID agents arranged to interview Yi late one night at the police station around the corner from the Kum Sung. They showed her photographs of the suspects and asked if any resembled the man in the hall.

Yi pointed to a photo of Nick Baer, the soldier who had danced with Kenzi and who said he only vaguely remembered Jamie.

"She stated she could not say Baer was the individual who she saw in the Kum Sung Motel. Yi related Baer most closely resembled the individual she saw," a CID investigator noted.

The Korean police told the Americans they were in the process of arranging for Yi to undergo hypnosis by a scientist at NISI. Perhaps she would remember more then, they said.

Back on MP Hill, the army investigators were zeroing in on Baer and another hasher, Mick Kolinski. Neither man had a firm alibi. Kolinski, the second man to kiss Jamie on the dance floor, said he was very intoxicated and stumbling around Itaewon at the time of the murder. Baer, who had danced with Kenzi, said he was wandering through the crowd at Stompers chatting with people whose names he either did not know or could not remember.

Now Yi was saying that Baer looked like the man loitering outside Room 103. He had olive skin and cropped hair like the man and was wearing khaki pants the night of the murder.

Kolinski did not have a dark complexion, but he did have the right shoe size. The hiking boots he handed over to the CID officers were size 9½.

The CID agents reviewed the videotapes from Stompers again and focused on the times that Kolinski and Baer appeared. The video was more *Girls Gone Wild* than security tape. The shots were randomly angled and jumpy. Scantily clad women jiggled up to the camera. Shirtless men danced on tables. The camera seemed to be passed from friend to friend, and often the frame was filled with people mugging for the camera. It was impossible to determine times or locations.

In one shot, Baer danced on a barrel with a young

Caucasian woman. Two weeks after the murder, they identified her as Natalie Langley, one of the leaders of the hashers. A preschool teacher from New Zealand, Natalie was celebrating her twentieth birthday the night of the murder.

She told the CID agents she had danced with all the hashers that night, including Nick. The agents pressed her for specific times, but she shook her head.

"It was over a four to five hour period, so you lose track of people," she recalled. She said the investigators wanted to know if either man or any of their hash friends had a bad temper.

It was laughable to Natalie. Stompers could be a scary place for single women. Prostitutes trolled the club for customers, and that led to a lot of drunken men to grope whatever they saw.

"The hash guys always stayed around the women in the group to protect them from that. No matter how late we would stay out, one of them would always be nearby in case anything happened," she said. "It was like a family."

Agents also interviewed Baer's co-workers, including his best friend, another hasher who was partying in Itaewon that night. The soldier told investigators he had gone home with a woman he met at Stompers around 3 A.M. He said when he talked to Baer the next day, he seemed his normal "mellow and goofy" self. The soldier said Baer bragged about doing "body shots" of tequila off the breasts of a woman who read weather reports on the army's news channel. When it turned out she was married, he moved on, the friend said. He said Baer told him he stayed at Stompers until 8 A.M. because "the party just kept going."

* * *

As they had promised the army investigators, the Korean police took Yi to NISI for the hypnosis that they hoped might jog her memory. Hypnosis is rarely used as an investigative technique in the United States but it is fairly common in Korea. Before the exam started, the technician asked the police if Yi had been shown any photos of possible suspects. Yes, they told him, the American army agents showed her four different lineups and she picked out one man.

That is unfortunate, the hypnotist told them. There's a chance she will describe the man in the photo and not the one in the hall.

He proceeded with the process anyhow. Under hypnosis, Yi gave police a more detailed description of the man in the hall. He was not Korean, African or Caucasian, but "mixed race."

"His face looked flat and he did not have much flesh and his cheeks were wide. He appeared to be nervous and awkward by the way he carried himself. His cheekbones were not high and he had thin facial features and did not wear glasses. The ridge of his nose was not high, and the end of the nose appeared to be dull," she said.

She put his height between five-nine and five-eleven, two inches taller than before, and changed her description of his shirt, saying it was not bright-colored as she had previously remembered, but either gray or sky blue with horizontal stripes around the chest.

Perhaps the most striking change in her hypnotized account was the gender of the motel manager. It was not the man, Sin, but his wife, Chong-Sun Pak, that she had seen in the lobby and heard yelling at the man in the hall.

For the Korean police, both of Yi's accounts raised questions about the statement they had taken from Sin the day Jamie was murdered. The motel owner never mentioned yelling at a man loitering in the hall, and he had assured officers that his wife knew nothing about the crime.

The Koreans confronted Sin at the Kum Sung, and after hedging for a few minutes, he made a stunning admission. He never saw a man with bloody pants. The night Jamie was murdered, he was out with friends gambling. It was his wife, Pak, who had been on duty and had seen the man rush from the motel.

He tried to explain why he had lied.

"My wife has a feeble mind and she is not mentally stable when she gets a shock," Sin told detectives. They were furious. They had worked the case in the belief that Sin was their most important eyewitness.

They took Pak to the Yongsan Police Station and began questioning her. She conceded she let her husband lie for her, but said it wasn't her idea.

"I just followed him," she said.

She told the angry officers, however, that her husband's account of the man with the bloody pants was not far off. At 3:30 that morning, she got out of her bed behind the window and walked into the hall. She was upset that her husband was not yet home and decided to wait for him in the lobby. As she walked toward the lobby, she heard a noise and saw a white man exiting Room 103.

He was wearing khaki pants, and as he moved past her she noticed there was blood on both legs. The right leg was soaked from the ankle to the knee and the left had blood spots "as big as a button," Pak said.

"I didn't talk to him, but I murmured to myself 'blood on his pants,'" she said.

She told the police that she got a good look at the man, and he was not one of her paying guests.

"He was a Caucasian man, round face," she told them. "I cannot recall his hair style but he was about 170 to 175 centimeters [five-eight to five-ten] in height, relatively short for a foreigner, a little bit chubby [in] build, wearing no glasses."

She said he was wearing a light jacket with a "checkered pattern shirt" and brown hiking boots. Pak said the man made a right turn out of the motel, the direction of the subway and Hooker Hill.

"I could recognize him [if] I saw him again," she told the police.

The Korean detectives questioned her about Yi's account of the man in the hall. Why were you yelling at this man? they asked.

Pak shook her head. I never saw such a man, let alone yelled at him, she said.

Yi saw you when she came into the hotel, they told her.

"No, she is not true. I believe she is not telling the truth," she replied.

The detectives quizzed her about others who had come into the Kum Sung that night, including Anneloes, Jeroen, Kenzi and Jamie.

She said she had not noticed any of them.

"All the rooms were occupied by customers [so] I didn't pay much attention to the people coming and going that night," she said.

Not even Anneloes? they asked. She claims she asked you for water.

No, she said, that never happened.

The Korean police were clearly frustrated with Pak and her husband. In one interview with her, they accused her of knowing who the man with the bloody pants was.

"You are not telling the truth because you do not want those people to be punished, and you are afraid of being punished because you have not been truthful on the case," the detective charged.

"That is not true," Pak retorted.

Convinced Pak was covering for someone, the detectives briefly focused on one of her grown children, a son who lived elsewhere in Itaewon. They asked her if her son frequented prostitutes or participated in anti-American protests or was gay. No, she told them. She said he didn't have keys to the rooms and had no reason to be in the motel.

CHAPTER 7

HOW DO YOU KNOW JAMIE?

Whatever their concerns about Pak, authorities behaved as though they believed she had seen the killer. They assembled a half-dozen soldier lineups and even brought her to a base for a face-to-face meeting with Martinez, who along with his friend Vincent had all but been exonerated. She said none of the soldiers she saw was the man in the hall.

Investigators also used Pak's description to develop a composite sketch of Jamie's killer. They posted it around Itaewon and at the entrances to the base.

The wanted poster described a male with "a well rounded, clean face shape," wearing "a fine check" shirt, beige pants and brown shoes, perhaps Timberland.

Inexplicably, the poster listed the suspect as about five-six to five-eight, shorter than Pak's description.

The sketch accompanying it showed a young Caucasian man with a crew cut. On a Saturday night in Itaewon, the sketch fit about three of every four men on the street.

Shortly after the poster went up, the CID got a tip about a private serving at an airbase just outside Seoul. The tipster said the private, a helicopter crew chief, was behaving very oddly the Monday after the murder. The soldier was telling people he had amnesia and did not know where he had been for the past forty-eight hours. The private, the tipster said, resembled the man on the wanted poster.

CID agents went to the base and interviewed the private's commanding officer, who confirmed parts of the story. He said he was concerned enough about the soldier to have him committed to a psychiatric ward on the Yongsan base. Not only had the private blacked out, but he was heard muttering about sabotaging helicopters. The officer said that ten days after he checked the private into the hospital, doctors there shipped him to Walter Reed Army Medical Center in Washington, D.C., for more psychiatric treatment. From there, the officer had lost track of the man.

Investigators were intrigued until they began reviewing the man's hospital records. The tipster was wrong. The private's mental breakdown wasn't the Monday after the murder, but ten days later. Agents talked to the private's roommate who told them that the soldier rarely left the barracks for leave and had only been to Itaewon once, a day trip months before. He wouldn't know how to find a club or a motel, the man said. He had mental problems, the roommate told them, but more than anything, he was trying to get out of the Army.

The dead end led the army agents to come back to Kolinski and Baer. One had the right shoe size; the other had the right face. But over and over, the soldiers denied ever setting foot inside the Kum Sung, let alone killing Jamie.

In an interview with the military newspaper *Stars and Stripes* later, a soldier who spoke under the condition of anonymity, but whose story and assignment clearly identify him as Baer, said that he told the investigators it was ridiculous to think he had murdered Jamie, a girl to whom he spoke "maybe three words."

He was interested in Anneloes, "the real cute one," not Jamie, he said.

Even as they hammered away at Kolinski and Baer, army investigators knew they had a nearly insurmountable problem in pinning the crime on either man. NISI scientists had gone over Kolinski's jeans and Baer's khakis with a magnifying glass. They had swabbed every crevice of Kolinski's hiking boots and Baer's Skechers. There was simply no blood.

Snapshots the hashers took in Nickleby's and interviews with people who crossed paths with the men left no doubt they had the right clothes. The investigators looked at the gory photos of Room 103. Blood was splattered on the walls and the floor. At the very least, the killer's boots would have been soaked with blood.

In perhaps the final blow to their case against the pair, Baer agreed to take a polygraph. He passed.

* * *

On April 27, 2001, a warm spring day about a month after Jamie's funeral, the University of Pittsburgh held a memorial service for her at Heinz Chapel. The Penichs drove in from Derry. In choosing the speakers, Dr. Yucas kept in mind the grief counselor's advice that what parents of a dead child need most is assurance the child will not be forgotten.

The university chancellor spoke first and called Jamie "bright, healthy, happy and hardworking" and "a person of vision."

"She will continue to be in our thoughts and memories and our prayers," he said.

Her academic adviser, Dr. Keith Brown, told those gathered that he was "still in the anger stage of her needless death.

"Jamie was precisely the kind of student every professor wants to see. She was using the college experience to its fullest, not just passing through," he said, adding, "She will be greatly missed."

The director of the day care center where Jamie worked announced they were creating a memorial garden decorated with stepping stones for the children.

"The stepping stones of Jamie's life ended rather abruptly, but I believe her spirit lives on," the director said.

Jeff Gretz spoke near the end of the service. As he looked out on the pews, he must have remembered that Jamie had wanted to marry him in that chapel.

"I do not know what Jamie is doing in the afterlife. I do know what she would not want to be doing. She doesn't want to be sitting on a cloud playing a harp. She wants to be doing stuff," he said.

He mentioned the goal she had told him about when they first met.

"Maybe she didn't change the world, but she changed the worlds of everyone who knew her," he said, his voice catching in his throat.

Dr. Yucas told the gathering that in tribute to Jamie, the university was planting a purple beech tree on the lawn outside the chapel. After the ceremony, Brown approached the Penichs to offer his condolences. The college world was an unfamiliar one to Patty, but she knew enough from Jamie to realize the professor's comments about her daughter were something special.

"You have so many students and so many classes. Why would you remember Jamie?" Patty asked.

"She just stood out," Brown replied.

Patty nodded.

To her family, it seemed like Patty's will had died along with Jamie. She had always been a great and enthusiastic cook, who delighted in whipping up elaborate holiday meals for dozens of relatives, but since March 18, she hadn't so much as turned on a burner.

"It was like 'Why bother?'" she recalls.

She closed the door to Jamie's room, leaving everything inside exactly as it had been the day her daughter left for Korea. She gathered up all the family snapshots and packed them away. It was too difficult to look at the pictures of Jamie beaming in front of the Christmas tree or grinning with all her cousins around the Thanksgiving table. The smiles just seemed so crazy. Couldn't any of them have seen what was coming?

But late that spring as the ridges around Derry

turned from gray to pale yellow and green, Brian and their daughters began to detect a slight thaw in Patty. She wasn't ready to talk about Jamie or what they all had lost, but she did want to know about the investigation.

Early on, there had been plenty of information about the search for Jamie's killer. The arrest of a soldier seemed just around the corner. The embassy called the Penichs frequently, and officials at the Korean National Police gave interviews to the Pittsburgh newspapers documenting the case's progress, but as April turned to May, the articles stopped and the phone calls from Korea became less and less frequent.

The Penichs began to sense the investigation was faltering. Sometimes their calls were not returned for days, and when they were, the family was told there was no news.

In Derry, they would have driven over to the state police barracks and demanded answers, but from the other side of the globe, there did not seem to be much they could do. They could not communicate with the Korean detectives, and the army did not give out information.

Television had once been a refuge from thinking about Jamie's murder, but as their frustration grew, it became an inspiration. Every true crime show or police drama contained hope for solving difficult cases. They began taking notes.

Did they check for bite marks? Did the coroner scrape under her fingernails? Did they look for fingerprints in closets in case someone was hiding there?

"We were trying to be our own little detective agency from over here," Patty said.

She began contacting the Korean police, the army investigators and the embassy. By her nature, Patty is shy. She is a small-town woman who married her high school sweetheart and lives a thirty-second walk from her mother. But the dearth of answers about Jamie's death made her suddenly brave.

"I'll call anyone now. I'll ask anything," she told friends.

She sent e-mail after e-mail and placed dozens of international calls. She had lists of specific questions. She wanted to know about forensic tests and interviews, and she even proposed a few leads of her own. Did the investigators know, for example, that Jamie had just received $1,000 in stipend money, money that was not sent back with the rest of her belongings? If one person did not have answers for Patty, she would call someone else. She would wait on hold, and if they disconnected her, she would call right back.

In mid-April, Jeff Gretz received a strange call from a consular officer at the U.S. embassy in Seoul. The man wanted to know Gretz's full name and date of birth. When he asked why, the man told him they were going to run his name through immigration to make sure he had not been in Korea at the time of the murder.

Go ahead, Gretz said, but to him and the Penichs, the call seemed an indication that investigators were far from finding the real killer.

One of the few official correspondences the Penichs received from Korea that April confirmed that. It was a letter from Woon-ha Hwang, a superintendent in the Korean National Police:

*I would like to express my sincere condo-
lences on your daughter being victimized in a
country so far away from home. I understand
that she was a beautiful and energetic young
lady who was curious to learn different cultures
and customs.* [The Korean National Police] *has
been doing our utmost to find the perpetrator.
We knew that finding the murderer would be the
only way to comfort the grieving family and
friends of Jamie, as well as the spirit of Jamie
herself, but unfortunately, we have not been
successful to date. One thing we want to reas-
sure you is that we are still continuing the investigation and that we will not give up or get
discouraged easily.*

Hwang noted the assistance of the army investigators
and then added, "In my business, we have a saying:
'There is no perfect murder.' We are determined to find
the person who did this."

Attached to the letter from Hwang was a two-page
document entitled "A Summary of the Investigation so
far." It had been translated from Korean and contained
many misspellings and grammatical errors, but for the
Penichs it was a trove of previously unknown information.

• *We have investigated enough the fellow including Anneloes and Kenzi in terms of the
incident happening and the recognition of the
criminal, but we couldn't find any clues from
them to solve the problem of this incident.*

- *We found the total 63 stuffs including a blood spot, hairs, pubic hairs, and others and requested National Institute of Scientific Investigation to examine them. The result is that the blood spot found there belongs to Jamie' own and hairs and pubic hairs Jamie's and Anneloes own. We found the foot-print that seem to belong to the criminal.*

- *We thoroughly investigated the total number of 25 people stayed in the hotel and recognized a guest who could see a person looked like the criminal in front of #103.*

- *After investigating the owner of the hotel, we found that the female owner witnessed a white man in beige pant with blood spots. We distributed the wanted montage by the information we found.*

- *With the recognition that Jamie spent a time together with unknown men in the bar, along with the U.S. CID we thoroughly investigated their alibi, shoes, and pants. Among them we focused on a man with a lie detector, but we couldn't find the criminal.*

- *In order to revive more accurate memory from the witnesses or female owner and a guest we tried to do hypnotism and based on their statement, we concluded the criminal may be a white man with normal body about 175cm tall.*

The Penichs flipped to the second page, titled, "A Future Plan." Beneath the hopeful headline, however, there were just a few lines:

- *We make a decision that there might be other people who haven't been recognized yet among the people joining together at the bar with Jamie and we will investigate all people being at the bar the day.*

- *We have a plan to broadcast the program asking people to report clues about the incident through SBS (Seoul Broadcast System), on the other hand we will spread lots of wanted montage in order to get a clue for the incident.*

The substance and brevity of the plan was astounding. So they were starting over from the beginning, looking for new suspects who had had a month to dispose of evidence and come up with alibis? And a wanted poster and some sort of Korean-style Crime Stoppers? Weren't these things that should have been done on the first day?

Patty's heart sank.

"They've botched this up real good," she thought.

Six weeks after the murder, army investigators made a round of visits to the five soldier suspects. If the GIs were expecting more questions or lineups, they were surprised. The agents handed each of them a bulky evidence bag. Inside, each man found the shirt, pants and footwear investigators had seized for forensic testing.

The agents offered little explanation.

"I don't remember if they ever told me I wasn't a suspect anymore," Mick Kolinski recalled. "I don't remember any part of closure."

On May 1, however, an army press officer told the *Stars and Stripes* that all military suspects had been cleared.

"There's no longer any U.S. Forces Korea personnel listed as suspects," the official told the military paper. "Everyone that has been identified as having anything to do or in the proximity to [Jamie] has been eliminated as a suspect that we are aware of."

The official indicated that without any GI suspects, the investigation would go back to being a local operation, with the CID assisting when the Koreans specifically requested it.

Since the beginning, *Stripes* was the paper of record in the Penich case. The Pittsburgh newspapers reported on the murder early on, but getting information out of Korea was difficult. *Stripes* had a bureau in Seoul, a staff of both Korean and American reporters and a strong interest in accusations of wrongdoing against soldiers. The daily paper is technically a U.S. government publication, but its editors are independent, and the content is not subject to military censorship or control.

Patty came to depend on the *Stripes* website for information about her daughter's case. That May, the paper wrote articles about the exoneration of the soldiers and the status of the investigation. Often the stories bolstered the Penichs' sense that the case was mishandled. The paper detailed problems at the crime scene, including police officers placing multiple pieces of evidence in one bag and the officers' inability to lift even a single fingerprint from Room 103.

Stripes reporter Jeremy Kirk also wrote that in some cases, CID agents had waited a week before seizing clothes of men who had been in the bar with Jamie and Kenzi. He raised questions about the wanted poster that Superintendent Hwang had touted to the Penichs. The poster didn't go up on base until a month after the murder, one soldier who had briefly visited Nickleby's told Kirk. By then, memories were fading.

Perhaps no information was more jarring for the family than the *Stripes* coverage of the semen test results. The paper reported that the police samples came back positive for the presence of semen. Much later, American investigators would deem the findings meaningless because they were done with an old-fashioned test that often mistakes routine infections for the presence of semen.

But in the stories Patty read, the lab director at NISI said that semen was found on Jamie's genitals and on two pairs of underpants: one belonging to Anneloes and the other belonging to Jamie.

"We cannot definitely say she was not raped," he told the paper. He cautioned, however, that the tests showed only trace amounts of semen, normally an indication that sexual intercourse occurred a day or two prior. The amount was so small that DNA testing was not even possible, he said.

Anneloes, however, protested the finding to the paper, saying that she had never had sex while she was in Korea and as far as she knew, Jamie had not either.

Complicating matters, the police superintendent said his reading of the results was that they were negative for the presence of semen.

The discussion upset the Penichs and reinforced their belief that their daughter's case was not in competent hands.

"We are about at the end of our rope," Patty told the paper.

In the midst of the family's growing frustration, Jeff Gretz reached out to Kenzi Snider. She was the last person known to have seen Jamie alive, and she knew the soldiers that he and the Penichs believed were the most likely culprits.

According to Gretz, army investigators contacted by the family said they didn't even know how to get in contact with Kenzi because she had returned to the United States. To prove that this was ridiculous, Gretz did a quick search for Kenzi on the Internet and immediately found an e-mail address.

Was this the Kenzi Snider who did study abroad in Daegu with Jamie Penich? he wrote.

Immediately he got a reply. Yes, Kenzi wrote. How do you know Jamie?

"I was her fiancé," he wrote back. "EX-fiancé technically, but . . . that's a WHOLE other story."

He told her that the police tried to get her e-mail address and phone number from the Penichs, but "no one was going to give anything away until they checked with you. I won't say anything either."

He continued:

> While I have a million questions at the same time, I don't know what to ask.

I've heard she was really fond of you and I hope you don't but I can understand if you feel some guilt kicking in with all of this. Please don't!! Anyway, if it would be cool, I would love to talk to you on the phone. A little more personal. (Granted we don't know each other at ALL!) but that's up to you . . . I mean . . . here you are getting a strange email from a complete stranger . . . but I'll give you my number. I'd be MORE than happy to call you to save you in toll charges, but if you don't feel comfortable with that . . . that is okay with me.

He gave her his number and signed off the e-mail:

Please take care,
Love,
Jeff Gretz

Kenzi called Gretz that night, and the conversation was lengthy and wide-ranging. The two discussed suspects and Jamie's behavior in the hours leading up to her death. The family was gravely concerned about the semen test results. In their discussion, Kenzi assured Gretz that to her knowledge, Jamie was not seeing anyone in Daegu and did not have sex during her time in Seoul.

The next afternoon, Gretz wrote, "You answered so many questions that were nagging at our minds for the past 2 months . . . things that we thought we'd NEVER know."

He wrote that he had phoned the Penichs when he got off with Kenzi and the information he had passed along to the normally stoic couple had changed them completely.

"Not only did Patty just start gushing with all these emotions (happy, anger, sad) that she had been holding in for the past two months, but Brian even TALKED☺. That is a big step for him (hee hee)," Gretz wrote.

He told her that she could pass his e-mail address on to Anneloes, but added, "I really don't have any questions for her per se . . . since most of what we wanted to know YOU were around for."

Gretz encouraged Kenzi to go online and read the *Stripes* stories. At the urging of the Penichs, he also told her she should consider contacting the FBI in Pittsburgh. The special agent in charge there was acting as a liaison between the family and the investigators in Korea. He included in the e-mail a copy of the wanted poster hanging around Itaewon.

"They probably didn't bother to show it to one of the key witnesses (YOU!!)," he wrote.

In the weeks that followed, Patty Penich also e-mailed Kenzi to thank her for her help.

"Jeff mentioned that you clarified what we had been suspecting about Jamie having no sex. I am glad you are helping us. Please keep us informed of any new developments," she wrote.

CHAPTER 8

DIXIE COLUMBO

When the Penichs saw Jamie off to Korea in March, Patty pulled out a pen and paper in the airport and asked for a return itinerary. Jamie was twenty-one, but she was still the little girl who told her mom to go home on the first day of kindergarten, and she was consumed with leaving, not with coming back. She humored her mother, however, and read off the flight number, arrival time and date of her return: June 11, 2001.

It was on that sad date that the Penichs went to Pittsburgh for a meeting that would change the course of the investigation. They drove into downtown, to the hundred-year-old gothic building that houses the city morgue and the offices of the Allegheny County coroner. The man who occupied that office was no nameless civil servant, but Cyril Wecht. Wecht was one of the elite group of national forensic celebrities, men like Henry Lee and Michael Baden who rose to fame because of the public's fascination with solving crimes using science.

From O. J. Simpson to JonBenet Ramsey to Laci Peterson, Wecht seemed connected to every high-profile crime in the country. If he wasn't a prosecution expert, he was a defense consultant or at the very least, a commentator on cable shows. On those programs, he was inevitably identified as "renowned forensic pathologist Cyril Wecht."

Shortly after Jamie's death, Wecht had contacted the family to offer his help. With their growing disillusionment at the pace of the investigation, the Penichs were ready to accept his offer. In his enormous office, Wecht listened as the couple recounted what they knew. They handed him the few documents they had: an English translation of the Korean pathologist's report and a sealed packet of autopsy photos.

Wecht looked at the materials and then shook his head. In his opinion, so much more should have been done at the autopsy. He told them that if the murder had occurred in America, it almost certainly would've been solved through forensics.

The most important thing that Wecht did, however, occurred after the Penichs had left for the long drive back to Derry. He picked up his phone and called the office of Pennsylvania's senior senator, Arlen Specter. The men knew each other. Both had studied the Kennedy assassination—Specter as a junior counsel to the Warren Commission in 1963 and Wecht as a member of the pathology panel of the House Select Committee on Assassinations in the late 1970s. Although they had clashed on the "single-bullet theory" of the president's death, Wecht felt the senator would be eager to help.

In his fourth Senate term, Specter was a powerful figure in Congress and a popular politician in the Keystone State. As a senior Republican senator, Specter had close ties to the White House, but was not afraid to break with his party on issues such as abortion. His committee assignments reflected his status: He served on Appropriations, Judiciary and Veterans Affairs.

Wecht's phone call reached the senator's office at an opportune time. Specter was preparing to go to Seoul later that summer as part of weeklong visit by a bipartisan congressional delegation.

In August, Specter and a delegation led by Senator Joseph Biden, the Delaware Democrat who chaired the Foreign Relations Committee, visited China and Taiwan.

After high-level talks with the Chinese president and Taiwanese leaders, the senators flew to Seoul to meet with then-president Kim Dae-jung. The meeting at the Blue House, the president's residence, was critical for the Korean government.

Kim was eager for the Bush Administration to enter into direct negotiations with North Korea, but the Americans wanted North Korea to end its long-range missile program. The North Koreans, in turn, wanted the United States to scrap its missile defense plans. Further isolation of North Korea from the international community was a terrifying prospect for the south. The border was just ninety miles from Seoul, and a missile attack by North Korea would kill millions of South Koreans in a matter of minutes. The more the United States engaged the dictatorship, the greater the chances for stability, they believed.

When the talks concluded, Specter asked for a moment alone with Kim. He told the Korean president that one of his young constituents had been killed in Seoul and that it seemed nothing was being done to solve the murder.

"Although he was not familiar with the case, he agreed to inquire about its status and work with the Korean police force and the American embassy staff on facilitating its swift resolution," Specter recalled a month later when he detailed his trip in the *Congressional Record*.

The mention of a grisly murder in a cheap motel must have been jarring in the Blue House with its pristine mountainside location and graceful, templelike architecture. The august residence was just a subway ride from Itaewon, but worlds away from a place like the Kum Sung Motel.

Kim must certainly have been embarrassed by Specter's comments. The talks with North Korea were vital to him, and one of the men who might persuade President Bush on his stance toward the Korean peninsula was now telling him that a young American girl had been brutalized here.

It is not clear what steps Kim took after meeting with Specter, but soon the Korean police, the embassy, the FBI and the army knew about his concerns. An FBI agent later described the subsequent pressure to make an arrest as "intense."

The army had stepped back from the case that spring, but a few weeks after Specter's visit, they assigned a new CID agent to lead the investigation.

* * *

At thirty-three, Mark Mansfield was one of the older CID agents on MP Hill. He was also one of the least experienced. At the time he was assigned to re-investigate Jamie Penich's murder, he had been an agent for just ten months, four of which were spent in training.

To an outsider, the selection of a greenhorn for a politically sensitive case may have seemed odd. The case was the most challenging and complex Mansfield had ever worked, let alone the only murder. His supervisors apparently saw in him more important attributes than investigative know-how.

One was likely his age. Many of the CID agents involved in the Penich case were as young as the soldier suspects and exchange students who were the key witnesses. Investigators in the CID hold a title outside of the rank system—"special agent"—so they can confront and interrogate more senior soldiers who would otherwise outrank them. But while differences in rank could be concealed, differences in age were more difficult to hide.

Mansfield carried a distinct air of maturity. He had served a decade in the marine corps before joining the army and spent two years as a military policeman before transferring to the CID. Detective work may have been new to him, but the armed forces and its personnel were old hat.

Mansfield's personality also worked in his favor. A native of Temple, Georgia, a town west of Atlanta with a population of two thousand, tinier even than Derry, he was friendly, charming and spoke in a warm Southern drawl that put people at ease and camouflaged his agile mind. He was openly devout and talked about his wife back in Atlanta and their three daughters, whom she was home schooling. With his good ol' boy demeanor, Mansfield seemed like sort of a Dixie Columbo, a smart policeman whose bumbling ways lured criminals into underestimating him.

Mansfield also had the respect of other investigators in the army and in the Korean police. He was regarded as the straightest of arrows. He didn't take shortcuts or shirk work. He didn't boast. He never swore or told crude jokes. His coworkers ribbed him about being a Boy Scout. He always shrugged it off with a smile. "My integrity is all I have," he would say.

Mansfield had the advantage of knowing the case without being steeped in the bad leads and dead ends. He had worked on the team of investigators questioning the students and tracking down soldiers in the days after the murder. He had talked briefly to Kenzi to get descriptions of Vincent and Harlan and had helped question Vincent.

But three days into the investigation, he had to leave Seoul for noncommissioned officers' school in the States. He did not return until late June, long after the soldiers were cleared.

Two months later, after the Senate delegation had left Seoul, Mansfield's supervisor assigned him to lead the investigation. He knew it was politically charged, and years later, he can still recall a moment where he realized that two important leaders had talked about a murder case that was now sitting in boxes in his small office.

Still, he insists, "there were never any discussions

where I was told 'You better solve this case because Sen. Specter asked the Korean president about it.'"

The pressure he felt came from himself, he recalls. He knew he did not have much experience, and the case had already frustrated investigators with much more detective work under their belts.

"I was intimidated," he said.

He bucked himself up and threw himself into reviewing the case file. The process took him nearly two months. He pored over the witness interviews, the autopsy reports and lab tests, the crime scene photos, the polygraph examinations, and the hypnotist's conclusions. He read the reports that army investigators before him had written. He saw how they had pieced all the evidence together and arrived at a sensible hypothesis— an amorous soldier, a spurned advance and an eruption of rage—only to have every possible suspect turn into a dead end.

After six weeks of combing through the case file, Mansfield sat down at his computer and typed out an e-mail to a person he believed knew things about the murder that were not in the case file: Anneloes Beverwijk.

From the first hour after the murder, there were questions about Jamie's Dutch roommate. Many investigators simply did not believe it was possible for someone to sleep through such a brutal murder, and Anneloes knew well that the American and Korean detectives harbored these doubts. The repeated suggestions that she knew more than she was saying angered her, and ultimately they led her to stop cooperating with authorities. Her parents, who had come to Korea after the murder to support her, and officials from the Dutch consulate persuaded her to cut off communication with the investigators after a week.

After she returned to Holland, reporters from *Stars and Stripes* and Korean television continued calling her for interviews. One question was always the same: How could you have slept through it?

What Anneloes did not know that fall was that Mansfield had taken steps to verify her story. He had arranged for detectives to interview the Korean woman whom Anneloes had roomed with during her brief stay at Keimyung. The Korean student confirmed that Anneloes was a remarkably deep sleeper. She wouldn't hear her phone even if it was on her pillow and she would sleep through her alarm every day, the young woman said.

Still Mansfield felt that she must know something more. She admitted waking up at two other points during the night—first when someone opened the door to her room and second when someone touched her shoulder. Perhaps there was some small detail she might not have mentioned. Perhaps she would be willing to undergo hypnosis?

Knowing that she was tired of having her story challenged, Mansfield approached her gingerly. In an e-mail written on September 26, he introduced himself and wrote, "I realize after reviewing your statements how much you have already tried to help in this investigation. I appreciate all the time you already gave, and I realize how difficult this whole thing must be for you.

"I am not contacting you to re-question you concerning all the dates and times you already provided," he wrote.

He asked if she would be willing to talk to him over the phone.

"Rest assured my only concern here is bringing the individual(s) who did this to Jamie into custody. All information, however slight, is so very important in this case," he wrote.

That fall, Anneloes was studying in the United States, but she immediately returned his e-mail.

"Mr. Mansfield, I am of course always prepared to help in the case, but I am really not sure how, since I did not really see anything," she wrote. She told him, however, that she would be happy to answer his questions. Just e-mail me, she wrote.

But Mansfield did not write to her that day or that week. Something had caught his eye and taken the investigation in a very different direction.

CHAPTER 9

STARTING OVER

Mark Mansfield loved order. He had joined the marine reserves immediately after high school graduation. He went in looking for college money, but he stayed in the corps because of the discipline. Every man doing his part. The entire organization running smoothly. He liked things to add up just so. His college degree, from a state school near his hometown, was in finance, and when he went on active duty with the marines, he worked as an administrative clerk, making sure records were kept exactly right.

After ten years in the corps, he left active duty. He was twenty-eight, with three young daughters, and the money was better in the civilian world. He got a job at a family-owned building materials store. He worked hard, as usual, and got promoted several times, eventually becoming a store manager at Lowe's, the national home improvement chain.

His supervisors loved him, and for the most part, his employees respected him. But Mansfield hated it. There were no standards as in the corps. Sometimes his workers showed up, sometimes they didn't. The goals, if you could call them that, were not lofty and fixed as in the service, but constantly changing and profit-driven. Sometimes he had to make ten cents on each two-by-four. Other times it was eight cents. The weather and traffic and the price of gas all affected sales. How could one man control who bought these things?

"I hated managing so many people and the lack of control. It's a tough job, and you can't really get your arms around the whole thing," he said. He found himself constantly comparing the work to what he had done in the corps.

"The military is something you can get your arms around. There are rules. There are ways of doing things. There is a standard," he said.

Within three years, he was back in the military, this time the army. When he reenlisted, he told them he didn't want to be an administrator anymore. He wanted to be in law enforcement, specifically a CID agent. For a man who craved order, it might have seemed strange to choose a career dealing exclusively with people and situations that were disordered. But Mansfield saw a CID agent's work as setting straight what was crooked. He wasn't interested in kicking down doors or roughing up people. He was interested in what he called "the entire process of discovering how or why something occurred and seeing justice served if possible."

In early October, Mansfield was scouring the catalog of evidence from Room 103 when he noticed something. Among the contents of Jamie's purse was a nametag bearing the name of Michael Greco, another American exchange student studying at Keimyung.

Greco, a nineteen-year-old anthropology major from the University of Rhode Island, had been invited on the trip to Seoul, but investigators were under the impression he had remained behind for a meeting with his host family. If that was true, though, why did Jamie have his nametag? Greco sounded like an Italian name. Maybe he was the young man with olive skin Yi saw in the hall or the dark-haired male Pak saw with blood on his pants.

Tracking Greco down was easy. He was still at Keimyung. He had been the only American to remain after Jamie's murder, and he had stayed on that fall for a second semester. Mansfield arranged to go to Daegu with the Korean detectives and an FBI agent named Seung Lee. Lee, a Korean American stationed at the U.S. embassy, would act as a translator between the groups.

The Korean investigators decided to bring Pak, the motel manager's wife, with them. If Greco was the killer, they reasoned, she would recognize him. In the United States, police lineups are regulated by strict policies designed to make sure the results are admissible in court. Generally, witnesses are required to select the suspect from among several people behind a one-way mirror or from an array of photos.

In Korea, however, witnesses are often brought face-to-face with a single suspect. The witness stares at the person in police custody for a few moments and then tells police whether they have the right suspect.

According to Mansfield's report, Greco got a Korean-style lineup in a conference room at the university on October 5, 2001. After looking the student over, Pak told the police "she was 99 percent sure Greco was the individual she saw outside Room 103 . . . who had been wearing the blood stained trousers," Mansfield wrote.

His report indicates the identification had an electrifying effect on the team. They spent hours questioning Greco afterward and found some of his behavior suspicious.

"Greco was extremely nervous at the beginning of the interview. He had accepted a cigarette from [Special Agent] Lee, but it did not appear that Greco was a smoker," Mansfield wrote.

Greco insisted he was two hundred miles away from Seoul in Daegu the night of the murder. According to their report, Korean detectives spread out across Daegu in search of witnesses to poke holes in Greco's alibi. Meanwhile, Mansfield arranged for Greco to take a lie detector test. The results indicated Greco was being "deceptive," according to the polygrapher's report. Mansfield turned back to Anneloes with questions about Greco's personality and his relationship with Jamie.

"Did you ever find Mike to have a temper or get angry and do you know if he had any interest in Jamie?" he wrote.

"I know he had to stay back in Daegu to meet with his host family, but that meeting was early in the day on Saturday. I was just wondering if he wanted to come up to Seoul after the meeting, and maybe [exchange student Elvira Makhmoutova] called him," he wrote.

The questions unnerved Anneloes. "I have never seen Mike having a temper or getting angry, and I don't think he had any special interest in Jamie. I have no clue why you are asking me these questions," she replied.

Mansfield's report suggests that within a few days, the investigators had come to agree with the Dutch girl. The Koreans had located many alibi witnesses who saw Greco in Daegu, and they couldn't make the train schedule work with the murder timeline. His roommate, Park, said he and Greco had eaten dinner with Park's family that night and passed a lie detector test to that effect. Park's parents and other witnesses also backed his story.

Park told them he never saw Greco display any real interest in Jamie. "If Mike saw a pretty female, he used to say that the female was sexy and he wanted to sleep [with her]. However, he never made such a comment about Jamie," Park said. "Jamie appeared to be scholastic," he added.

Ultimately, investigators concluded Greco failed the lie detector test because he had talked extensively with the other exchange students about the details of the case. He had nothing to do with the murder, they decided.

The Daegu experience severely shook investigators' faith in Pak. Did she know what the killer looked like? Or were all young Caucasian men the same in her eyes? Had she simply seen Greco with the officers and said whatever she thought they wanted to hear?

Frustrated, and now apparently faced with doubts

about an important eyewitness, Mansfield searched for a new approach.

"I was starting over," he later testified.

In his office on MP Hill, Mansfield stared at the case file. Its thousands of pages seemed an enormous collection of wrong turns, bad leads and unproven theories. The only way to solve this, he thought, is to go back to the first day and forget everything that came after. He tabbed through the file to the first folder, the statements of the exchange students.

"I decided I would go back to the beginning with the students and kind of scrub the reports, all the statements, and see if there's something I'm missing as far as soldier interaction, anything that I had missed," he later explained.

He was spreading the papers out on his desk in thin piles—Jeroen here, Anneloes there, Kenzi there—when he noticed a dark mark on the rear of one of the pages. He flipped it over and saw a heavy black boot print. He turned it back over. It was a page from the first statement Kenzi had given the Korean National Police the morning of the murder.

He picked up the phone and called Lee, the only FBI agent in Seoul.

"I think I've got something. Can you come here?" he asked.

Later, when everything was over, Lee would tell people he had been nothing more than a glorified translator. As a legal attaché at the embassy, he was a diplomat, not an investigator.

"I had no business being involved in this case," he would say with a smile.

The truth, however, was that more than any army agent, Lee was Mansfield's right hand in the reinvestigation of the case. After Specter visited Korea, the U.S. ambassador called Lee into his office. He had a stack of letters from the Penichs, and now a senator was breathing down his neck.

This Penich case, he said. Is there anything you can do to help?

Lee shrugged. He had never worked on a murder investigation, but he wanted to be accommodating.

I speak Korean, if that might help, he said.

It seemed a simple thing, but in short order, Lee's language skills made him instrumental in the investigation. When Mansfield interviewed Americans, like Greco, Lee was there to translate for the Korean National Police. When the Koreans interviewed natives, Lee was there to translate for Mansfield.

Straddling the two worlds was familiar to Lee. He had lived in rural southern Korea until he was sixteen and his mother, who was the town nurse and midwife, decided prospects for Lee and her other two children were better in the United States.

She settled them outside Washington, D.C., where she got a job as a nurse's aide. Lee found himself in a large American high school in the mid-1970s. He knew only a few words of English, and the ways of American teenagers were even more mysterious.

He taught himself English by listening to old Beatles records and working side-by-side with native speakers at after school jobs. At the University of Maryland, he pursued a degree in accounting and worked nights at a liquor store. He struck up a friendship with a regular customer, an FBI agent. The man persuaded him to apply to the bureau.

"I didn't know what the FBI was, but I thought it sounded neat," he recalled.

After a brief stint as an accountant, Lee was hired in 1984. He spent the next fifteen years in counterintelligence. He worked on teams trying to catch traitors and spies sent by other countries.

"It sounds exciting, but it was mostly mundane. The things we do to investigate—they are very organized, based on empirical evidence. You would be bored," he said.

In July 2000, Lee's assignment changed when the bureau decided to open its first office in Korea. Lee was the obvious choice. It was an exciting move for him and his wife, a Korean American, and two preteen daughters. The Korean press celebrated his arrival. A native son in the FBI!

The principal of his middle school in Korea asked him to speak to the students. He remembered the school as a primitive place in a poor rural region. When he arrived, he was stunned. The Third World of his memories was gone. The students were healthy, and they wore Nikes and listened to Walkmans.

"It had changed. A lot," he remembered.

Lee settled into the relatively humdrum life of an FBI legal attaché. He was the sole employee of his office, so he answered the phones, filed the paperwork, filled out his own expense forms and even emptied the trash. The work was routine. He did background checks on prospective employees and lent a hand in the occasional cyber-crime investigation that had a Korean connection.

The Penich murder was far and away the most interesting thing to cross his desk, and the more he learned about the case, the more he was drawn to it. One of the biggest reasons was Mark Mansfield.

Lee had known a lot of good investigators in twenty years at the bureau, but he liked no one better than Mansfield. Mansfield was smart and hardworking, but had no ego. He never cut corners or snapped at colleagues. He looked everyone in the eye and gave him respect.

The two cut an odd pair. Mansfield was six feet tall and trim with a crushing handshake, a big smile and an abundance of Southern charm. Lee was shorter and starting to get the paunch of a man who spent his days at a desk. He wore sport coats and slacks that didn't always match. He was soft-spoken and reserved.

The pair complemented each other well. Lee knew Korean society, Mansfield knew the army.

When Lee arrived at MP Hill, Mansfield showed him the print. The paper was a copy of one of the stilted interviews Kenzi had done with the Korean police interpreter. The Koreans had made a Xerox of it for the army case file. The boot print showed the treads of a heavy boot like the one that killed Jamie.

"Is it possible they took a boot print from Kenzi and this is it?" Mansfield asked Lee.

Let's go ask the Koreans, Lee said.

The two drove to the Yongsan Police Station. In the detective bureau, Mansfield excitedly placed the paper down in front of his Korean counterparts.

The Korean detectives stared at it and then burst into laughter.

You think this is the smoking gun, they said, shaking their heads. This isn't her print at all.

They explained that immediately after the murder, they bought boots of all styles and treads and slathered their soles with ink. They then pressed the shoes onto sheets of copy paper. The ones that didn't match, they had sent to the copy room for recycling, and by chance, the recycled paper was used to copy Kenzi's report.

Some big break, the Koreans jeered. Lee thought that if he were in Mansfield's place he would've told the Koreans to shut up and stop being nasty, that he was just doing his job and they should be more understanding. Instead Mansfield just thanked them politely for straightening him out and smiled. The detectives could still hear the Koreans laughing as they left the stationhouse. They drove back to MP Hill in silence.

On the surface, it was another dead end. But something about it kept nagging at Mansfield. On the way to the police station, he had thought about Kenzi. Could she have somehow been involved? The Korean police were right about the inky boot print, but maybe he was right about Kenzi.

Later, Lee would think that the result of the dead end had been worth all the humiliation at the police department.

"What it did was get our minds on Kenzi once and for all," Lee recalled.

CHAPTER 10

THERE WAS NO SHOWER

When he went back to MP Hill, Mansfield picked up Kenzi's statements. For the next two months, he rarely put them down. He read them over and over. He took them with him to the Kum Sung Motel and to Nickleby's bar. He kept them by his side when he interviewed new witnesses. He made charts based on them. He read parts of them aloud to Lee. After eight weeks, he convened a meeting with the Korean police and announced a shocking new prime suspect: Kenzi Snider.

Mansfield's conclusion must have stunned the Korean detectives. Kenzi Snider? The sweet, blond teenager who had provided the most useful information in the early days of the investigation? The one who burst into tears when she talked about Jamie? The one who called her mother "mommy" on the phone?

Sure, she had been testy during some of their interviews, but none of them had blamed her. She didn't like being told she knew more than she was telling, and anyone would get irritated with inept translators.

Are you sure? they asked.

With Lee at his side translating, Mansfield told them he based his conclusion on Kenzi's own words. She gave investigators at least five statements about St. Patrick's Day night. He said he combed through them and found they contradicted one another, other witnesses and the evidence. Just hear me out, he told them.

Two months earlier, when Mansfield began scrutinizing Kenzi's statements, one part of her account immediately struck him as odd and possibly suspicious: her description of going back to check on Jamie in Room 103 before turning in for the night.

She told the Koreans and the Americans that Jamie was quite drunk and having trouble walking. When they returned to the motel, Jamie wanted to shower to sober up, so Kenzi had helped her undress and turn on the water. In a statement to the Korean National Police the day of the murder, she said:

I asked Jamie if she was ok, and she said yes. I left the room and went back to my room. When I got inside my room, Jeroen was sleeping on the outside of the bed away from the wall. I got into bed and after a minute or two, I decided to check on Jamie. I went to her room, knocked on the door and asked her if she was ok and she replied

*"yes." I didn't check the door and I went back to
my room.*

To Mansfield, the account was nonsensical from the
start and got more unbelievable the closer he looked.
Kenzi was worried enough about Jamie's welfare that
she got back up out of bed after a couple minutes to
check on her. But when she got to the door to Room
103, she didn't go in or even stick her head inside to
verify that she was okay? It was a lot of effort to go
through not to even lay eyes on Jamie, he thought.

Mansfield picked up Jeroen Kuilman's statement.
The Korean police had questioned him very briefly
since he had not met any of the soldiers in Nickleby's,
nor heard anything unusual from his bed in Room 104,
directly next to Jamie's room. But one thing in his short
statement immediately grabbed Mansfield's attention.
He told the police that he woke up only one time, when
Kenzi opened the door to Room 104 and crawled over
him into bed. It was around 3:30 A.M., he told the detectives.

Kenzi was a large woman, and the bed was small for
two people, Mansfield thought. Even if she were trying
not to wake him, it would have been difficult, maybe
impossible. It was a cold night, and there were covers
to arrange and rearrange. She had to lift the blankets,
throw herself over Jeroen, and replace the blankets. If
she had done that three times in the space of a few
minutes, why did he remember only one time?

Mansfield decided to test her statement with what he
would later call a "nonscientific test." He grabbed another CID agent and drove off base to the Kum Sung.

Jamie Penich

(Penich family photo)

Jamie *(left)* and Kenzi in a snapshot taken on the weekend trip to Seoul

(Court File—Seoul High Court)

The Kum Sung Motel *(right, foreground)* is located on a side street in the Itaewon District.

(Court TV)

The door to Room 103, the room Jamie shared with Dutch student Anneloes Beverwijk

(Court File—Seoul High Court)

Only a few inches separated Jamie's body from the bed where Anneloes said she was sleeping at the time of the murder.

(Court File—Seoul High Court)

Korean police were the first to arrive at the motel. Later they would be criticized for carelessness at the crime scene.

(Court File—Seoul High Court)

A page from the autopsy report details the substantial injuries Jamie suffered.

(Court File—Seoul High Court)

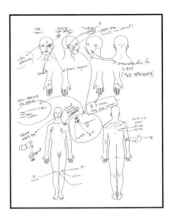

As this police photo illustrates, Jamie's clothes were found in the bathroom and her naked body just outside it.

(Court File—Seoul High Court)

Police found a smudge of blood on the circular knob on the door leading out of the motel.

(Court TV)

This crime scene photo of Jamie's jeans and underwear on the bathroom floor piqued Mark Mansfield's interest.

(Court File— Seoul High Court)

The black fleece jacket that covered Jamie's head was marred by a bloody footprint.

(Court File— Seoul High Court)

When Jamie's body was discovered, there was a plastic bag in the bathtub.

(Court File—Seoul High Court)

Jamie with her older sister, Jennell, and younger sister, Amanda

(Penich family photo)

Brian and Patty Penich in the living room of their home in Derry, Pennsylvania

(Court TV)

Jamie Penich's headstone in St. Martin's cemetary in Derry. It reads: "If tears could build a stairway and memories were a lane, we'd walk right up to heaven and bring you back again."

(Court TV)

I'm remembering more, but I still don't know how long it took.
We were arm in arm walking home. We got into the room. She unbuttoned
my plaid shirt and drops in in the corner. She checks on Anna and says
we have to be quiet. (Inserted by Snider) She took off her shoes and shirt in
the room. She takes my hand and we walk into the bathroom.
I don't know who turned on the light. She's by the tub. She takes off
her bra. (Inserted by Snider) She takes off her bra, jeans and underwear.
She takes my hand, pulls me closer and we start to kiss.
I don't know how long we're kissing. I start playing with her chest. I kissed
down her stomach. She's still standing and I go to kiss down there. I don't
know how long. We kiss a bit more. She kinda pushed me back. She
moves her arms around me and is playing with my waist. She's going for
my button. I move away. I'm thinking no but I can't get it to come out.
She goes for the button again. I hit her hard. She's in the bathtub. She
looks hurt. She's quiet. She hit her head. She looks uncomfortable. I don't
mean to hit her, but I'm mad at her. I'm angry. I go to pick her up. She's
heavy. I trip and she falls. Her head hits the floor. We're outside. I trip on
the thing in the floor. I'm mad at her. She's still unconscious. I pick her up
and move her again. She doesn't make me feel any better. I'm hurt and I'm
angry. I don't want her looking at me. She won't stop looking at me. I
don't know why, and I pick up my foot and it's heavy. I don't know how
many times I hit her. I don't know how many times. And then I just stare at
her. She's not looking anymore. I just stare at her. I don't know, but I pick
up a jacket (Inserted by Snider) I didn't know it was jacket, and cover her
head and she's not looking anymore. And I just stare. I don't know but I
pick up my shirt and I go and lock everything out. I lock my door to lock
everything out. I didn't mean to.

Q: SA MANSFIELD
A: SNIDER
Q: Where are you standing while your using foot?
A: I'm above her. I'm above Jamie. Anna is behind me.
Q: The item you discussed as stepping on, where is it?

Part of the confession Kenzi Snider dictated
to Mansfield on February 6, 2002

Kenzi leads Korean investigators through Itaewon as part
of her reenactment of the murder.

(Court File—Seoul High Court)

During the reenactment, Korean police provided a mannequin to represent Jamie at the Kum Sung Motel.

(Court File—Seoul High Court)

Kenzi and her mother, Heath Bozonie, speak to reporters after her second acquittal.

(Court TV)

Kenzi Snider

(Court TV)

He told Pak and Sin he wanted to see Room 103. You can, they told him, but only if you rent it. Fine, he said, and plunked down a few won notes.

Mansfield went into the bathroom, closed the door and started the shower. The second agent closed the outside door to Room 103 and stood in the hall.

In his report, Mansfield wrote, his colleague "made the statement 'Are you OK!' and SA Mansfield responded with 'Yes.' It was the opinion of both agents that it was very difficult to hear what was being said by each other. Further, each agent was listening for a statement and response, and Penich would not have been expecting Kenzi to return and ask if she was OK."

Back on MP Hill, Mansfield was convinced Kenzi was lying about that part of her story and began scouring her account for other contradictions. He looked closely at her description of Jamie undressing in the bathroom. Kenzi maintained Jamie was unsteady on her feet, so she had helped her disrobe.

"I took off her shirt in her room and took off her blue jean pants in the bathroom. I remember that I threw her blue jeans in the floor of the bathroom," she told the Koreans.

She said that when she left Room 103, Jamie was standing outside the shower in her bra and panties.

In a book of crime scene photos, Mansfield found what he considered absolute proof Kenzi was lying: a photo of Jamie's clothes in a pile on the bathroom floor. The picture clearly showed that Jamie's panties were inside her jeans and the jeans were on top of her bra. She took her shirt off, then her bra and then stepped out of her jeans and panties in one motion, he thought. She was never standing in just her underwear. Another lie from Kenzi, the agent thought. He began to wonder what exactly had happened in Room 103 after the bar.

He focused on her statements about Vincent, one of the mysteries of the case. She said he waved to her on the street as she helped Jamie back to the motel. CID agents had grilled Vincent about this encounter for hours, but he insisted that he did not see her outside the bar. The streets were crowded and I was drunk, he told the officers, I may not have seen her if she walked by, but I am positive I never waved to her.

Mansfield wondered if Kenzi was trying to incriminate Vincent. In the first interviews, she described how he had hit on her in a booth and invited her to come home with him in exchange for a free trip to a tropical island.

"I told him no, but he was insistent. Finally, I told him I had to go," she said in her initial statement.

Vincent admitted that he had invited her to come away with him to Jeju Island and that she had turned him down, but he described it as less confrontational. Just another Saturday night in Itaewon, and another girl to hit on, he recalled.

Kenzi had described Vincent in more alarming terms two months after the murder in an interview with *Stars and Stripes*.

"He was very strong and forward and very fast, and I didn't feel right with him," she said of Vincent. In an FBI interview that summer, she described him as "sexually aggressive."

"He asked her to sleep with him that night. She turned him down, and the conversation bothered her, so she climbed over the table to get out of the booth . . . Vince seemed a little annoyed at the declination," the interviewing agent wrote.

Vincent told investigators that account wasn't true. The bar was crowded, but he wasn't holding her captive in the booth.

Mansfield also considered a statement she made to Korean police a few days after the murder about another suspect, Nick Baer. Kenzi noted that Baer was manning the pitchers of green beer at Nickleby's and said she thought Jamie's inebriation might stem from something he put in the drink.

In the statement, awkwardly rendered by a translator, Kenzi said, "Nicolas offered us a lot of drinks in the Nickleby's Club and further Jamie could not get up in her room. It was because I guess Nicolas added something to her drink. I wish you interview Nicolas more deliberately."

Lab tests had shown Jamie was free of drugs, date-rape and otherwise. Was Kenzi deliberately trying to place blame elsewhere?

Lastly, there was the issue of time. Nearly everyone investigators interviewed that night, including Kenzi, said she was drunk and did not have a great sense of time. Initially, Kenzi said she and Jamie had left the bar sometime between 2 A.M. and 3:30 A.M. She later told authorities that after talking to the other exchange students and reflecting further, she thought she and Jamie had departed about 3:15 A.M.

As Mansfield saw it, that was problematic. Kenzi said she and Jamie had left the bar about the time the hashers had moved on to the nightclub. The hashers were very intoxicated and leaving in groups, but they put the time they left for Stompers between 12:30 A.M. and 2 A.M.

Mansfield went back to Itaewon and reinterviewed the bar owner, a German expat. The American girls left about 1:30 A.M., the man said. Can you be sure? Mansfield asked. The man acknowledged that it was a busy night and he wasn't keeping tabs on people.

Is it possible that she left at 3:15 A.M.? Mansfield asked.

Absolutely not, the owner said. He said that by that time, the hashers were gone and the bar was empty except for a dozen people. The American girls were not among them, he said.

So if they really left at 2 A.M., Mansfield wondered, *and Jeroen felt her crawl into bed at 3:30 A.M., what was going on in between? And why is Kenzi lying about it?*

Mansfield ticked off the list of contradictions to the Korean investigators at a meeting in December 2001. Lee translated, and the Koreans seemed open to his findings. He told the detectives that he wanted to talk to the men who had been at the Kum Sung crime scene the morning of the murder. He wanted to know if they noticed anything that pointed to Kenzi.

The detectives set up a television to watch a brief video of the crime scene. As the camera panned over the bathroom, Mansfield pointed out Jamie's bra underneath her jeans and underwear.

The camera swept over to bathtub and lingered on a plastic shopping bag resting on the bottom of the tub.

"I wanted to know what the plastic bag was doing

there, because Miss Snider had stated that Miss Penich had taken a shower," Mansfield later recalled.

"They said there was no shower. And I was puzzled and I said, 'Well, what do you mean? There must have been a shower.' They said, 'No, there was no shower. There was no water,' " he said.

The tub was dry and so was the bathroom floor. Mansfield pressed them about crime scene photos that showed Jamie's hair was damp and a report that stated her jeans were wet. Her hair was soaked with blood, not water, and the jeans were damp in only one spot, the Koreans explained. Mansfield was dumbfounded. Perhaps the water had simply evaporated.

He returned to the Kum Sung and once again rented Room 103 for a "nonscientific test."

"I put a measurable amount of water, small amount. I took the [shower head], sprayed the ledge of the bathtub, the ledge of the floor," he recalled.

He returned six and a half hours later—about the time between the murder and the processing of the crime scene.

"About half the water was still there," he said.

She lied about this too, he thought. It was time to confront Kenzi Snider.

CHAPTER 11

ROOTING FOR THE HERD

Kenzi Snider had no idea that autumn that she had become the prime suspect in Jamie Penich's murder. As Mansfield built a case against her, she was back at Marshall University in West Virginia, slogging through her junior year.

Eleven days after Jamie's death, she had left Korea for St. Cloud, Minnesota, where her three older brothers lived. Her mother had returned to her teaching job in Thailand, and St. Cloud, a city of sixty thousand on the prairie an hour northwest of the Twin Cities, was the closest thing she had to a hometown.

Her parents had grown up in Minneapolis, and during a rough patch in their marriage, her mother purchased a bungalow in St. Cloud and enrolled in the state university there. Kenzi lived there from fourth to seventh grade and then again in tenth, when her parents finally divorced. In her mind, St. Cloud had only ever been a pit stop between better places, and this trip was no exception.

She was happy to see her brothers, but she made sure everyone knew it would not be long before she was off again. As she had predicted in the letter she wrote to Jeroen while still in Korea, she found the concerns of her brothers and friends smothering. They were worried about what she had experienced in Seoul and peppered her with questions.

She briefly escaped to Huntington that spring. She met with the study-abroad director at Marshall. She told him she felt a little guilty about coming home so soon from Korea. She knew that as the first Marshall student to study there, she was setting a bad precedent, but she simply couldn't stay after the murder.

Her teachers and classmates at Marshall were also curious and concerned about her time in Korea. She soon found their queries as oppressive as the ones in St. Cloud.

"I'm thankful that people cared, but when you are asked 'How are you' all the time, you can only pretend for so long. You'll say you are okay, but you are not really okay," she recalled.

Less than a month after she got back to the States, she left for the Netherlands. She spent three weeks visiting Anneloes and Jeroen. She said they mostly "hung out," occasionally talking about the murder, but primarily enjoying not being asked if they were okay.

"We could be not okay together. Or we could be okay and not feel that that was wrong," she later recalled.

She returned to St. Cloud late that spring. Until fall, when she could reenroll at Marshall, there was nothing for her to do. She stayed in her mother's bungalow with her twenty-three-year-old brother, Roman, who was working as a cook in a restaurant. Both siblings knew they would be moving on soon, and they did not bother to decorate or unpack. The place felt like temporary housing rather than a home.

Kenzi spent evenings with the few other young adults she knew from her brief stints in elementary and high school. A group of them worked together at the Target store. They liked to visit the bars and coffeehouses in St. Cloud's tiny downtown.

Kenzi was always up for getting together. For the most part, she was still the bubbly, kind girl they remembered from grammar school, always game for an afternoon at the coffeehouse or a beer.

But even in these lighthearted moments, it was clear the events in Korea were foremost in her mind. When she and some girlfriends went to see the film *Moulin Rouge*, Kenzi bolted from the theater mid-movie. In the lobby, she told them that something on the screen caused her to flash back to the murder.

"I know it was really troubling her. The thoughts kept coming into her head," one friend, Jennifer Thompson, recalled.

She would occasionally refer to a recurring nightmare. She confided to Roman that one question about the murder nagged her day and night: Had she twisted the little knob on the door of Room 103 to the lock position when she left Jamie?

"It always came back to did she lock the door or

didn't she," he said. "If she locked the door, then what had happened to Jamie wouldn't have happened."

She spent hours that summer on the Internet tracking case developments.

"She was always on the computer, looking stuff up about it," Roman recalled.

Her friend Anneloes had stopped answering questions from the press, but Kenzi was always willing. When reporters from *Stars and Stripes* called, she never refused an interview. She learned as much from them as they did from her. Kenzi had stopped getting information from the Korean police and the army agents the day she left MP Hill. The results of lab tests, the accounts of Pak, Sin and Yi, and the soldiers' full names and specific alibis were tightly guarded investigative secrets. When *Stripes* reporters managed to shake some information free, Kenzi was eager to hear it and to serve up some new information of her own in exchange.

In one e-mail in late May, she told reporter Jeremy Kirk that in addition to the five known suspects, she had recently remembered someone else. "It could just be my mind playing tricks on me, but I am almost positive there was another man named Clint," she wrote.

It was about the same time she was quoted in a *Stripes* article as describing Vincent as very menacing and scary.

"I'm not afraid to talk to reporters or as unwilling to answer questions," she explained later. "I know [the other exchange students] said they wanted to get their life back and move on but for me, answering the questions is how I'm moving on."

She kept up her e-mail and phone conversations with Jeff Gretz, Jamie's former fiancé. They discussed theories and new developments. Toward the end of May, Gretz forwarded Kenzi an e-mail from Patty Penich. The subject line was "Nick."

Patty wrote that she had talked to a reporter at *Stripes*.

"Nick is in the U.S. on 30-day leave. He has two weeks left. His name is Nick Baer," she wrote. She instructed Gretz, "Tell Kenzi."

That night, Kenzi told her brother that she was terrified.

"She thought [Baer] was going to come and get her," Roman Snider recalled.

She said that he looked most like the composite sketch on the wanted poster. She had also discussed with Gretz a theory the Penichs had: that the killer was looking for Kenzi, but stumbled into Jamie's room instead since it was closer to the front door. Kenzi had spent more time with Nick than Jamie. She seemed a more likely target.

The day after she got the e-mail from Patty, Kenzi walked into the FBI office in St. Cloud and told them she had feared Nick Baer might try to harm her. The agents in St. Cloud's small field office knew absolutely nothing about Jamie Penich or her murder, but they wrote a six-page typed report. The report covered everything, from her arrival in Daegu to the trip to Seoul to how she helped Jamie get ready for bed after the bar.

"Penich said she wanted to take a shower before she went to bed and to sober up some so she would not wake up with a hangover. She steadied Penich as she got undressed down to her bra and underwear," the agent typed.

The last three paragraphs concerned her current state of mind:

> She had replayed the events the night of the murder in her head many times and it all seemed so bizarre. Everything seemed to be friendly and fun. It was a jovial atmosphere. There was never any indication that anybody was mad at Penich or that Penich had done anything to upset anyone. She had no strong suspect but thought that Vince and Martinez had the best opportunity because they were the only ones who may have been able to follow them back to the motel. However, she never saw Penich with Vince at the bar and had not seen Martinez at the bar at all.
>
> She had heard that Nick became a strong suspect based on a statement from the motel office clerk who said she saw a man with tan trousers that had blood on them leave Penich's room early that morning. She [Snider] saw a composite drawing of the man as described by the motel clerk and thought the drawing looked like Nick. Before hearing of the motel clerk's statement, she had not suspected Nick because Penich and Nick only danced together a couple of times and there was no hint of trouble. Further, they never saw Nick again after they left Nickleby's Pub and he did not know where they were staying.
>
> She, Penich's boyfriend, Jeff Gretz, and Penich's family were upset with the pace of the investigation. She spoke with Gretz frequently over the

*telephone and also learned pieces of information
about the investigation from on-line articles . . .*

Baer never contacted Kenzi, but the FBI in St. Cloud
faxed the report to Lee in Seoul, and he sent it on to MP
Hill. Months later, it would be one of the statements he
compared to build a case against her.

Huntington, West Virginia, stretches along the south
bank of the Ohio River near the bend where the Mountain State knocks against Kentucky and Ohio. Although
it is West Virginia's second largest city, it is quite small,
with just fifty thousand residents. Its low buildings,
quiet streets and valley setting make Huntington feel
more like a sleepy town than a city.

It owes its existence to the coal industry. Railroad tycoon Collis Huntington built the city at the spot where
the train tracks that brought bituminous coal out of the
mountain mines met the river, where barges could transport the coal to cities to the west and south.

It is a five-hour drive from Derry, but the two have
common Appalachian traits. They are insular, remote
places with many citizens who cannot imagine living
elsewhere. Both areas prospered when coal was king,
shrank with its collapse and still struggle economically.

Huntington defines itself by Marshall University and
its sixteen thousand students. Outside West Virginia,
the school is best known for a 1970 plane crash outside
town that claimed the lives of seventy-five people, including most of Marshall's Thundering Herd football
team. Inside the state, Marshall is respected as one of

two large public universities. Eighty percent of those who enroll are from West Virginia, and the student body mirrors the state's population: overwhelmingly white and rural. Many are the first in their family to attend college. With a grade point average of 2.0 required for admission and annual tuition under $4,000, Marshall is an accessible, affordable place for West Virginians.

Kenzi learned about the university when she was thousands of miles away from the wooded ridges of western West Virginia. She was in high school in Kuwait when a teacher who was an alumna recommended Marshall. A state school deep in Appalachia might have seemed a poor choice for a cosmopolitan young woman who had lived around the world, but from the moment she set foot on the campus, Kenzi declared herself in love.

She had spent a childhood blowing across four continents. Where she went and how long she stayed was always up to her dad, her mom, an ambassador, or the air force, but never her. Finally she was alone and could stay or go at will. In West Virginia, people stayed. We don't like to be too far from our kin, the friends she met at Marshall explained.

She went home with them for holidays and weekends and saw that their families had lived for generations in the same valleys and coal towns. Her schoolmates planned to plow their degrees back into the rocky soil of the state. They were amazed that she had lived so many places and done so many things, but it was not a life they envied.

For Kenzi, their view was as fascinating as that of any far-off culture. Home didn't have to be a flexible term. Away did not necessarily mean better. She still talked about following her mother's path and teaching abroad, but she began mentioning other, more grounded, aspirations as well.

"I remember her telling me once that this was the one place she really felt at home and at peace with," a friend, Eugene Johnson, said later. "She wanted to go out of the country and teach, but this was the one place she wanted to buy a house and keep a home here to come back to."

At the end of the summer of 2001, Kenzi was thrilled to return to Huntington. She registered for a full schedule of classes and moved into a small apartment off campus. Her friends and some of her professors knew about the tragedy in Korea, but she did not volunteer information.

Clark Egnor, an administrator in the university's international studies center, had kept in close contact with Dr. Kim at Keimyung in the days after the murder. He worried that Kenzi, the youngest in the exchange program, would be the least equipped to handle the impact of the death. That fall he was particularly worried about how she would adjust. When classes began, he sought her out to see how she was.

"I felt so bad for her that she had had that experience," he recalled. He encouraged her to keep a busy schedule "to keep her mind off of it" and proposed she train to be an English-as-a-second-language tutor for foreign students at Marshall. She agreed.

"I would occasionally ask her did she hear anything about the girl from Pittsburgh, but she didn't have any news. She seemed okay, though. She wasn't jumping up and down happy, but she was functioning, she was taking classes," Egnor remembered.

Kenzi had always been a good student, and that autumn was no exception. She maintained her 3.81 GPA and earned a place on the dean's list. In class, her professors saw the same outgoing and enthusiastic student they remembered from her freshman and sophomore years. In Janet Dozier's Curriculum and Methods education class, Kenzi turned in assignments that were insightful and creative.

"She had a good grasp of the material and was willing to take a risk in conversation," Dozier recalled.

When the September 11 attacks occurred, Kenzi was in Dozier's class. The professor went from student to student offering whatever comfort she could. When she got to Kenzi, she thought of Kenzi's trip abroad the previous spring and her family's wide travels.

"I can remember telling her that I was so glad that she was home and that she was safe," Dozier recalled.

That fall, Kenzi took a part-time job at the Barboursville School, a residential treatment center for troubled teenagers. The school is a state-run facility with twenty-two beds for what its principal describes as "the worst of worst in the state of West Virginia."

All the residents are placed at the school by court order, and most have been kicked out of homes and schools. Some struggle with hallucinations and all are medicated.

"They all have DSM-IV psychiatric diagnoses, the preponderance of them are bipolar with explosive tempers," principal Charlie Buell explained.

The students spend the day in closely monitored

classes and then return to locked cottages for the evening. Kenzi worked as a "cottage counselor," escorting students to classes and making sure they did not run away.

The students she supervised would often bait their wards with foul language and violence. Counselors were trained in physically restraining out-of-control students. While the residents' outbursts would defeat some new employees, Kenzi seemed to thrive. She greeted the chaos with kindness, Buell recalled.

"She is just calm and didn't ever seem to lose her patience," he said. Administrators would often call her in for special assignments, including monitoring one twelve-year-old boy who refused to behave in school. He would stand up at his desk in the middle of class and do karate kicks until teachers removed him to a time-out room. One of Kenzi's jobs was to sit outside the room encouraging him to settle down. The boy was eventually removed to a facility in another state, but Buell, whose office was near the time-out rooms, was struck by the depth of compassion and patience Kenzi showed.

"Some people, the kid goes 'fuck you' and their instant reaction is an inappropriate one," Buell said. Not Kenzi.

"She would have been one of the more mature, more calm young people we have had working here," he said.

The almost saintly patience and good humor Buell noted in Kenzi were traits people often commented on in her. The most abnormal thing about her, in fact, seemed to be her lack of negative qualities. She was never mean or even curt. She smiled at everyone. She rarely complained. She was open to new people, but never needy. She was self-confident, but not arrogant. She never lost her temper.

Not surprisingly, she assembled a large group of friends at Marshall. She seemed incredibly independent to them for living alone and choosing a school so far from her family, but everyone was struck by her devotion to her friends. She spent hours listening to their problems and wrote them encouraging notes at exam time. She occasionally left flowers outside their dorm room doors. Together, they enjoyed the normal parts of Marshall life: drinking, dating and rooting for the Herd. On Sundays, Kenzi went to services at an evangelical church in Huntington. She also attended the church's weekly Bible study for college students.

Kenzi spent a lot of time talking to Jamie's ex-fiancé, Jeff Gretz. Their e-mail and phone conversations about the investigation soon turned into talks about life in general. The bond, Kenzi says, was Jamie's murder.

"His friends in Pittsburgh either didn't know her that well or that way. I had no friends where I was staying who knew Jamie or had any friends be murdered or die on them. We just had that common bond. We could talk about memories we had of her and the investigation. Because although people were interested, it's a different kind of interest," she said.

In September she visited Jeff in Pittsburgh, sleeping over at his apartment. In October he drove to Huntington to see her. She says the relationship was never anything more than a very close friendship.

CHAPTER 12

A LEGITIMATE SUSPECT

Mark Mansfield knew the logical next step in the investigation was to confront Kenzi Snider, but he also knew that he had no right to do so. The army began investigating Jamie's death because its soldiers were suspects. By pointing the finger at Kenzi, he had effectively taken himself off the case.

One American killing another in a foreign country was certainly unfortunate, but it was not a matter for the army. It was up to the locals to solve. Proper procedure required Mansfield turn over his notes to the Koreans and get back to the regular work of a CID agent, investigating bar brawls in Itaewon and drug use in the barracks.

But Mansfield just didn't see how he could do that.

The case was under his skin. After all these months of hard work, how could he just leave it to the Koreans? Some of them were dubious about Kenzi's involvement, and even if he could convince them, he doubted they could close the case.

There's no way they are going to go to America to question her, Mansfield thought. Even if they do, they won't be able to grasp the nuances of culture and language to properly interview her.

Mansfield had seen the stack of distraught letters the Penichs had written to the ambassador and the Korean National Police. He thought of his own daughters. *Am I going to be the one to just let this case die?* he wondered.

He told Lee how upset he was. The FBI agent knew Mansfield was right. "We knew the Koreans couldn't do it. Kenzi had been back in the States a year, and if we didn't do it, it was not going to get done," Lee recalled.

He was scheduled to return to Washington, D.C., in late January for a conference. He made Mansfield an offer: If you can get the CID to spring for an airline ticket, I'll get an FBI polygrapher and get us all to West Virginia to talk to her.

"Miraculously," Lee remembers, "the Army came up with the money." He and Mansfield were off to America.

As they boarded the plane, however, there was still a giant hole in Mansfield's theory: motive. Kenzi and Jamie were friends. The other exchange students saw them together hours before the murder and they were happy. Snapshots taken at the bar bore that out. What reason could Kenzi have for murder?

In Seoul, Lee and Mansfield spent hours discussing

possibilities. They kept returning to what they referred to as "the lesbian angle." Neither woman was known to be gay, but they were young and adventurous, the men thought. Maybe the murder was some sort of sexual experimentation gone wrong.

It was "the only thing we had developed that could possibly have caused that much rage out of Miss Snider," Mansfield later explained.

Jamie's nudity suggested sexual activity had occurred or was about to occur. Both women had been drinking, and the bar was a sexually charged environment. They were dirty dancing with soldiers. Jamie kissed two men, Kenzi kissed one.

Lee decided to run the scenario by a profiler at the Behavioral Analysis Unit, a section of the FBI Academy made famous by the movie *Silence of the Lambs*.

"I had a simple agenda. I wanted to know if what we were thinking was foolhardy or a legitimate possibility. Did they have to be very much of a homosexual to do what we think happened?" Lee recalled.

"We just wanted to know if we were off the deep end," he said.

Despite its mystique, the offices of the Behavioral Analysis Unit are about as nondescript as the regional office of an insurance company. The unit is housed in an office park along a busy roadway in suburban Virginia. The seven profilers in the adult division work on the second floor in tiny modular offices a half step up from a cubicle. If it wasn't for the framed photos of George W. Bush and FBI Director Robert Mueller in the lobby and shelves lined with binders labeled "Sadistic Homicide" and "Sexual Murders/Serial," the men and women hunched quietly over their desks might be actuaries.

When Seung Lee came to the office in late January 2002, he was looking for a favor. The profilers' time is precious, and getting one to work on a case requires a lot of paperwork and permissions and clearances. The Penich murder wasn't a bureau case or technically even an American case, but Lee was eager for reassurance on the lesbian theory before they met with Kenzi in West Virginia.

A few months before, when servicemen still topped the list of suspects, he had sent a packet of materials to profiler Mark Safarik for analysis. Translating the Korean police reports and photo captions into English took weeks, however, and by the time Safarik could examine the case file, Mansfield had started the reinvestigation that would lead him to Kenzi.

Now Lee was knocking on Safarik's door for some help with their new theory. Safarik, a supervisory special agent, had been in law enforcement for two decades. He had studied all sorts of different murders, though his specialty was the serial rape and murder of elderly women. He was busy, but he was willing to help Lee out, especially because he'd already reviewed the case. Lee began to fill him in on the new theory.

The first thing that Safarik had noticed when he reviewed the file was the way Jamie was killed. As manners of death go, stomping is exceptionally rare.

"Stomping is not the weapon of choice for most perpetrators," Safarik explained.

"If you see that sort of up close and personal type of attack, it is usually with hands. So you get strangulation or blunt force injuries caused by fists or a combination of fists and feet, but feet alone is pretty unusual," he added.

A stomping death assumes that the perpetrator was filled with rage, but did not have a weapon such as a gun or knife at hand. He may resort to using his feet because the victim falls down or because hands alone are not enough to inflict the type of damage desired.

In Safarik's experience, victims of stomping could be either male or female, but the perpetrators were always male, perhaps because of the strength required. To stomp someone, an assailant must first knock them down to the floor and men are more likely to be able to force someone to the ground with their hands or fists. Still, Safarik thought, there was no reason that a tall, large woman like Kenzi could not force a slight, short woman like Jamie to the floor.

He drew Lee's attention to the jacket that was on Jamie's face when her body was discovered. It was a piece of evidence that had struck him when he had first reviewed the crime scene photos months before.

This is very important, he told Lee. He explained that in the profiling world there were two types of behavior by killers at a crime scene. The first was modus operandi—MO. It was anything the offender did to avoid detection.

"Criminals want to be successful. They don't want to be caught, so they engage in behavior that protects their identity and helps them get away with it, anything that puts time and distance between them and the scene," he said.

A killer might choose a target that won't be missed right away, like a prostitute. Killers will lie in wait, hide bodies, and wear gloves; stage crime scenes to look like suicides or robberies, clean themselves up before leaving or to make a quick getaway.

The MO reveals some things about the killer to the profiler, but not nearly as much as the second type of behavior, which is known as ritualized or need-based behavior. It is anything the offender does that is not designed to make him more successful at getting away with the crime.

"It's generally stuff that takes place afterwards, like postmortem sex or posing the body or mutilation," he said.

"The more you interact with the crime scene the more chance there is that you will leave evidence or be detected, so the best thing to do would be to leave quickly. If the offender doesn't do that, it reveals something about him, his mindset and his relationship to the victim," he said.

Safarik pointed to the jacket. This is need-based, he told Lee. Whoever did this should have just left the room after killing Jamie, but they took the time to cover her face, Safarik said.

Covering a victim's face is normally an attempt to objectify and depersonalize the victim.

"Why do you need to objectify her?" Safarik explained. "Because you are uncomfortable with what you have done. That to me suggests some level of relationship between the victim and the offender, and I would not expect to see that with a military guy who did not know this girl."

Safarik told Lee that the jacket over the face went hand in hand with the lack of defensive injuries on Jamie's hands.

"By the time she recognizes she is in trouble, it is too late," he said. "That typically does not occur with a stranger and it doesn't typically occur where you have an escalation of violence," such as unwanted sexual advances, he said.

Curiously, Safarik and Lee did not talk about the saliva on Jamie's chest in their discussion of need-based behavior at the crime scene. Korean detectives and the army investigators had been convinced that the killer spat on Jamie as a last insult as she lay dying. But spitting seemed at odds with the positioning of the jacket. The jacket pointed to a killer who knew and respected Jamie and regretted the murder while spitting indicated a complete disregard for her and even pride in the attack.

Lee, however, was focused on determining whether Kenzi was a viable suspect and the conversation turned toward the lesbian theory. Safarik agreed that it was possible. The atmosphere of the bar, the experience of being away from parents and community, the alcohol, and two young heterosexual women might experiment, Safarik agreed.

"I walked away from that meeting thinking that we weren't doing anything totally stupid, that she is a legitimate suspect," Lee recalled.

Armed with the profiler's assessment, Lee phoned Kenzi at Marshall.

"They were furthering the investigation, and they wanted to speak to me as the last person who had seen her," Kenzi recalled. She told them she'd be happy to help.

On February 3, 2002, the two detectives hopped a puddle jumper to Charleston, spent the night and drove west the next morning through the mountains to Huntington. On the drive, they were excited and nervous. Neither knew Kenzi well. Lee had never met her, and Mansfield had talked to her only briefly a year before. They discussed their strategy for dealing with her.

"The most important thing was that she still thought of herself as the key witness in the investigation," Lee recalled. She was to meet them after her day shift at the Barboursville School, and Lee and Mansfield agreed that they would probably need more time than that evening to confront her.

"We were going to make it so that on the first day at least she still thought of herself as just a witness. Because we anticipated that it was very important to have her back on the second day, and that if she knew we were looking at her as a suspect she wouldn't come back," he explained.

As he had promised Mansfield in Seoul, Lee had arranged for a bureau polygraph expert to come to the interview. Marc DiVittis, a lie detector specialist from the Cleveland field office, was not familiar with the case, but Mansfield and Lee wanted him there to polygraph Kenzi if she insisted on her innocence.

It was an interesting trio. Mansfield and Lee knew the case backward and forward, but neither had ever investigated a murder. DiVittis, on the other hand, was a highly experienced investigator who questioned suspects in serious crimes every day, but didn't know the history of the case or the evidence.

The three men checked into the Ramada Limited by the interstate. Kenzi had agreed to meet them at 6 P.M., and Lee and Mansfield had time to sketch only the broad outlines of the case for DiVittis.

Just before she arrived, Mansfield and Lee sat in their rental car in the parking lot of the Ramada. They had traveled a long way to confront Kenzi, and now here they were, minutes away. "We were asking each other, what do you think? Could Kenzi have possibly done this? The answer was we don't know," Lee recalled.

CHAPTER 13

THIRD CULTURE KID

The Ramada Limited was five minutes outside town near the highway entrance ramp. It was a three-story, mid-range motel between a Wendy's and a Super 8 motor inn.

Kenzi was a few minutes early for her interview. She was accompanied by a girlfriend from Marshall, a fact that immediately disconcerted Mansfield and Lee. She explained to the agents, who had been waiting for her in the lobby, that it had been a long time since she had talked to authorities about the murder and she was worried about how it might affect her emotionally. I'm not sure what shape I'll be in when I leave, and I might need her to drive me home, she told them.

Mansfield and Lee said they understood, but that

they wanted to speak to her alone. That's fine, she replied. The agents told her that they wanted to interview her in the motel's conference room, but another group was already using it.

Is it okay if we just talk in Agent Lee's room? they asked.

Of course, Kenzi replied. Her friend sat down in the lobby, and Kenzi and the agents headed for the elevator and Room 226.

DiVittis was waiting inside. He introduced himself as an FBI agent, but not a polygrapher. The room was large, about twice the size of a room in the Kum Sung, with a big window that looked out on a back parking lot and beyond that a wooded hillside.

It was already dark, and as the agents had discussed beforehand, there was not enough time to confront Kenzi with their suspicions. Instead they concentrated on establishing a relationship with her—what Mansfield termed "rapport-building."

"My intent that night was just to get to know her a little bit, set her at ease as far as what was going on here," he later testified.

Each of the agents took turns showing Kenzi their badges, and then Mansfield and Lee began chatting with her about the fallout of the case. Mansfield told her that Jamie's murder was eating away at him. He was so intent on solving it that he was neglecting his own family, he said.

"He said he wanted to get this finished with so he could go back to his family and go back to his job and continue his life," she remembered later.

Kenzi sat in a chair by the window, nodding in sympathy. He asked her how she had been sleeping.

"I said I hadn't been sleeping very well. I mentioned that normally I used to dream regularly," she later recalled. Since leaving Korea, she told them, "I'd only had about three dreams that I could remember."

Mansfield asked about the dreams, and Kenzi described one in which she found herself in a large body of water.

"I was being attacked by a shark and a train at the same time from different sides," she said.

DiVittis, who had been silent up to that point, spoke up.

"He mentioned that for a female dreaming about a train, it's a sign of sexual conflict," Kenzi recalled later.

They asked her if she ever thought about the killer and if she believed she had talked to the murderer. Yes, she said.

Who do you think it is? Mansfield asked.

Nick Baer, she replied.

We looked at him as a suspect, but . . . Mansfield shook his head.

He and Lee asked her what she thought was keeping the killer from admitting what he had done. Every day must be so horrible, keeping this terrible secret, they said. Why not just confess and get on with life? Kenzi nodded in agreement.

"I don't know why they wouldn't want to," she said.

Lee said that the killer was probably a foreigner and that if the person had already left the country, it would be difficult if not impossible for the Koreans to extradite. And even if they somehow managed to, the person would be looking at a very short sentence. The system is different, and Americans get special treatment, he said.

He cited the case of an American soldier, Christopher McCarthy, who had strangled a prostitute in Itaewon in 2000 and received a sentence of just six years in prison.

At 8:30 P.M., Kenzi asked if she could go check on her friend in the lobby. They were supposed to have dinner later, she explained. When she returned, the agents told her they wanted to set up another time to talk.

What are you doing tomorrow? they asked.

She told them she had to work at the Barboursville School in the morning, but could come by at 3 the next afternoon.

Before she left, Mansfield gave her what he called a "homework assignment." He asked her to write out one more account of the events leading to Jamie's death. The agents were worried that Kenzi might have intuited their suspicion and decide not to return. They had no way to compel her. They were all outside their jurisdictions. The interview was voluntary. Because Kenzi had expressed a desire to help them, the homework was a way to ensure that she would come back.

During the three-hour interview, the issue of a lie detector test was not raised, and DiVittis never even brought his polygraph equipment to the room. The move was to become controversial. DiVittis would later say that the fact Kenzi brought a friend to the motel was proof that she did not trust them and would bolt at the mention of a polygraph.

Lee recalled it differently. He remembered that DiVittis made it clear he could either participate in confronting Kenzi or give a polygraph, but not both. "Once you accuse, you lose" is a maxim in the lie detecting community. An interrogator cannot call a suspect a liar and then administer a polygraph. The results will be worthless. Lee and Mansfield decided that given their limited experience, DiVittis was more valuable leading the interview than giving a polygraph. They had to keep Kenzi talking, and he was better prepared to do that.

As it turned out, the agents' fears that Kenzi was on to them were totally unfounded. She never imagined she was a suspect.

"We were joking and laughing, and I started to trust them. They seemed like nice gentlemen," she said.

Their questions about how she was dealing with Jamie's murder especially touched her.

"It's easy to trust someone if they sound concerned about you," she said.

By the time she got back to her apartment from dinner, it was late. She knew she had to be up at 6 the next morning for work, but she wanted to finish the homework assignment. She sat down on her bed with a pen and a stack of looseleaf paper and began writing out yet another account of her trip to Seoul.

Sitting alone in a motel room at night with three male government agents would intimidate—or at the very least, make uncomfortable—most twenty-year-old American women. But Kenzi Snider had never been much like her peers in the United States.

Whenever her parents' peripatetic life led back to the United States, people always commented on her uniqueness. She's so mature, so articulate, so independent, so self-confident, they would tell her parents.

Heath and Roger Snider just shrugged. It was the norm for a TCK—a Third Culture Kid. The term, coined by an American academic raising her sons in India in the 1940s, refers to the children of diplomats, missionaries, military personnel, business executives and anyone else bringing up a family abroad. These youths hold a passport for their parents' homeland and may even have been born there, but live in another country or in a series of other countries. Although they are familiar with their parents' culture as well as the culture of the places they reside, they are said to exist in a third culture of diplomatic compounds and international schools.

Kenzi and her three older brothers, Jordan, Durham and Roman, never knew another life. Heath and Roger Snider moved abroad before they were even married and stayed, at first to accommodate Roger's career in the air force, but later because they enjoyed living a different sort of life than their friends and family back in Minnesota.

The two had grown up next door to each other in Minneapolis and began dating in high school. In college, Roger enlisted in the air force and was stationed in England. Heath joined him, and they were married there. As a Morse code signal operator, Roger could work at any base, but he found international assignments more challenging than positions stateside. From England, the Sniders went to Japan, and by the time Kenzi was born in 1981, they were living in Brindisi, Italy.

Heath, a creative, energetic woman, thought life outside the States was less materialistic and more spontaneous. With a change of scenery, even the life of a housewife was exciting. There were always interesting people coming through the bases or the embassy, and navigating everyday life in a new place could be an adventure.

When Kenzi was a newborn, she fell out of her crib, fracturing her skull. It was scary, but Heath tried to make the best of it by concentrating on the differences between American and Italian hospitals. The food, the demeanors of the nurses, the doctors' bedside manners—it was all fascinating to her.

The Sniders' relatives did not always understand.

Heath's mother, a dressmaker in Minnesota, once chided her about her grandchildren's nomadic lives.

"You aren't giving your children roots," she said.

Heath shot back, "They have roots, they're just in pots."

Her father left the air force when Kenzi was a preschooler. Roger Snider says the decision was made in a fit of pique. He and his commanding officer disagreed about whether he should be sent back abroad as he wished or kept at home. When he came in a half pound overweight at his annual physical, his CO ordered him to lose the weight before his next assignment, he says. It was humiliating given his fifteen-year career, and he opted for a discharge instead, he says.

He eventually found a job that would allow the family to continue living abroad. He took a position in the State Department as a communications officer in overseas embassies. The family was sent to Belgium, and Kenzi enrolled in the local public kindergarten, where classes were conducted in French. She became bilingual in a matter of weeks.

Supporting six people on the salary of one civil

servant was not always easy, but the Sniders, led by Heath's unwavering enthusiasm, concentrated on what they had: one another and the experience of living abroad.

"Money was never a big issue with us. We used to make our own Christmas cards together, and we made our own gifts. We cooked together and did the yard together and laughed together and always ate dinner together," Heath recalled.

As the seat of NATO, Brussels was filled with uniformed officials, and the Snider children grew comfortable with them. When the children wanted to visit their father, they clamored up to the uniformed marine at the embassy gate and asked to see "daddy."

After two years in Belgium, Roger Snider was transferred to Zaire, the central African country now known as the Democratic Republic of the Congo. The family moved into a house on a hill outside Kinshasa.

The Snider children enrolled in the English-language international school. Her brothers were old hands at being the new kids, and Kenzi, then a second grader, learned from them and her Third Culture Kid classmates. TCKs had to make friends quickly. They had to walk into a classroom full of strangers in the morning with a big smile and a lot of confidence so that by lunchtime they would have someone to eat with, and by the end of the day, they'd have a group to walk home with them.

TCKs didn't have time to sit back and let friends come to them. They didn't have the luxury of waiting a semester before choosing a club or sports team. Classmates were coming and going every semester or even more frequently. If you waited a year to join Girl Scouts, your dad would probably be sent to some other country and you would end up in some other international school, and you'd be right back where you started.

Kenzi quickly mastered the art of making friends.

"We'd be somewhere a week and she'd have two best friends," recalled Jordan, who is nine years older than Kenzi.

The international school was a rainbow of races and nationalities, the children of diplomats, engineers, business people, and the occasional wealthy native. What the Sniders and the other children shared was a blasé attitude toward change. Countries came and went, friends came and went, language fluency came and went. For a TCK, the only constant relationships were with one's self and one's immediate family. That made for children who were introspective and vastly more mature than their peers at home.

Those who have studied TCKs say that the defining part of these children's Third Culture identity is a sense of always being an outsider. For some children, this means never feeling at home, but for many others, it means feeling at home in any situation. Kenzi seemed to fall into the latter category.

"She was usually the lead in the play and usually the math marathon winner, and she usually won the spelling bee. She could do a lot of things and she could do a lot of things well, and so when she went to see the principal, it was 'you won an award' or 'congratulations,'" her mother recalled.

Heath encouraged her children to be self-sufficient. When they would come to her with a problem, she made them define the precise issue, and then they had to come up with three different solutions.

"Now you need to pick the best solution, and if that doesn't work, you've still got two solutions to follow through," she would tell them.

The day-to-day life in Zaire was much different than that in Europe or Japan. The nation was ruled by the dictator Mobutu Sese Seko, and expats tended to live insular lives in what Roger Snider remembers as "rose-colored glasses."

"You might hear how bad Mobutu is to his people, but you don't see it and there's limited papers in English, and the local papers certainly don't carry that type of news. You just stick to certain confines and don't look at the other side," he said.

It was in the close quarters of Zaire that Kenzi's parents' relationship began to shake.

"Africa put a lot of pressure on the marriage. We had one car and there wasn't public transportation. We always had to be together," Jordan said.

Kenzi's father spent long hours setting up secure communication systems between the embassy and Washington, D.C. When he was home, he seemed perpetually in a bad mood. "He was moody, sullen, and didn't do anything he didn't want to," Kenzi recalled.

Her mom began wondering if they should've ever left the air force. And she wished she had a career of her own. At embassy functions, the Sniders could put on a good show, but back in the house alone, they were miserable. He and the boys fought, but Kenzi said her father rarely spoke to her.

"He kinda ignored me a lot. We never had a close

relationship. It was never like I was his princess or I was his only daughter. I was the fourth kid and that was it," she said.

After school, she would play in the house until her father arrived home from work. The minute she heard the door, she slipped out the back and stayed away until the streetlights flickered on below in Kinshasa—her curfew to be in the house.

Her brothers stayed away as well.

"We had a tendency as dad started getting angrier and angrier to just try to get out of the way, to just put his energy into something else," Durham said.

When Roger Snider was posted to Haiti, the family decided to split up. Heath took Durham, Roman, and Kenzi and went back to Minnesota. Roger took Jordan, the eldest, and flew to Port-au-Prince.

For Kenzi and her brothers, returning to America proved the most foreign experience yet. Her mother wanted to get a teaching degree and chose St. Cloud State. She bought a small house and enrolled the children in public school. The first day was a culture shock. Kids, even young ones, knew a lot about money and clothes and spending. They were less mature and thought nothing of speaking out of turn or otherwise disrupting class. Classes were less advanced than the Sniders were used to, and the students seemed wary of the new arrivals.

When the Snider kids talked about where they had come from or their adventures abroad, other kids accused them of lying or told them to stop bragging. After Kenzi's brother Durham got into a fistfight with a kid who did not believe he was born in Japan, Heath went to the school and gave slideshow presentations to each child's class about their lives before St. Cloud.

Kenzi, just a fourth grader, noticed subtle differences. "Abroad, if the door knob breaks in my hand, we would say, the door knob broke. In America, we say, Kenzi broke the door knob," she remembered thinking.

Heath was a full-time student, and money was very short.

"I think of it as the poverty years. We were on food stamps, but I didn't want the kids to know," she remembered.

Friends from the Unitarian church invited them over for meals and gave them clothes. Kenzi, however, focused on school. Her teachers delighted in her enthusiasm. Her scrapbooks from those years are filled with awards and photos of school projects and Girl Scout outings.

After three years apart, her parents decided to try to make the marriage work one last time. The family joined Roger in Dhaka, Bangladesh. Kenzi loved being back in an international school. She quickly made friends and learned about her new home. For a few weeks, her parents seemed happy, but by the end of the school year, it was clear things were not improving. After a brief stint in Florida, the couple divorced, and Kenzi and her mother returned to St. Cloud. Kenzi spent tenth grade at the local high school.

"She was so much more mature than any of us," Dan Roeder, a classmate, recalls. "At the time, I'd never even been outside of Minnesota, and she'd lived in all these interesting places."

Kenzi again noticed a lot of the things she disliked

about American schools. The bullies and disorder on the school bus bothered her enough that she took a city bus to school.

In class, she exuded a self-confidence that some students liked and others hated.

"She instantly became a best friend, or they really didn't care if they ever saw her again," Cassie Roeder, Dan's wife and another classmate, remembered.

"I think it was because she didn't conform. She was who she was and she didn't try to impress you. It was take it or leave it, whereas a lot of people in high school were trying to be like everybody else," she said.

By then, Kenzi had already decided that she wanted a career in education, maybe as a high school principal or counselor.

"She was so willing to share her dreams and goals. We thought of high school as this thing we were stuck in the middle of, but she could see it as her future. She was just ahead of us," Dan Roeder recalled.

After a year in Minnesota, Kenzi's mother was eager to get back to living abroad. She found a job teaching at a boys' school in Kuwait. Durham and Roman were staying behind, and for the first time, it would be just her and Kenzi going abroad. As mother and only daughter, the two had always been close. The boys openly referred to Kenzi as "mom's favorite." Going to Kuwait increased their already strong bond. After decades as a housewife, Heath had survived her difficult divorce and was finally an independent person with a career. Kenzi was on the cusp of young womanhood and thrilled to return to a life abroad, where her peers would be smart, worldly and kind.

Kenzi enrolled in the American School of Kuwait and began adjusting to a country far different from any she had lived in before. In the Muslim kingdom, the government controlled every school, even the private ones. All textbooks and teaching materials were subject to its approval. Pages concerning the Holocaust were cut out of history books. Inflatable globes would be returned to teachers deflated because government censors cut Israel out of the map.

Kenzi and her mother arrived at a time of tension between Iraq and the United States over compliance with weapons inspectors. American troops were streaming into Kuwait, and there was concern Iraq might try to attack. In Kenzi's school, there were drills for chemical weapon attacks. Children were given gas masks, and at the embassy, Americans were instructed that should there be an attack they would be whisked to the desert by army troops and then onto an aircraft carrier in the Persian Gulf.

The U.S. military bases were the hubs of social life for Americans in Kuwait. The expats went there for exercise, meals out, shopping and church. Kenzi began attending an evangelical church on base, mostly to meet people, but she was inspired by what she heard, and in the spring of her senior year, she told the church leaders that she wanted to accept Jesus Christ and be born again. She must have been one of the few people ever to convert to Christianity in Kuwait. From her time on the base and at church, she knew the embassy officials and the army brass as pals more than as authority figures.

"When you are overseas, authority figures are the moms and dads of your friends. You see your authority figures at the club, you see authority figures at the commissary, you have them over to your house, you play with their children," Heath remembered.

"There was no fear. There was just a sense of us being protected," she said.

Despite the winds of war, high school life was fairly normal. In her junior and senior years, Kenzi hung out with friends at fast-food joints in Kuwait City. They talked about who liked whom and where to go to college. The country was officially dry, but some students hosted discreet drinking parties with alcohol made from secret home stills.

Kenzi's school was filled with the children of sheiks, high-level diplomats and oil executives. She was one of the few poor kids.

"Our mothers sort of stood out because they were single and teachers," said Erin Lambert, Kenzi's best friend in Kuwait. Her mother also taught at the American School.

"We had less money. Our moms made our clothes and made their clothes. It wasn't terrible or anything, but we were aware of it," she added.

Kenzi dated a Canadian senior year, and they went together to the prom. Her mother made her a "Cinderella" dress with yards and yards of blue silk. The photos from that night show Kenzi smiling next to a tall young man in a tuxedo. Her strawberry blond hair is swept into a chignon, and a black velvet ribbon encircles her neck. Kenzi and her date are standing in a nondescript banquet hall, and nothing in the picture indicates it was taken in Kuwait. She looks like a typical American promgoer, happy and trying to look glamorous.

Looking at the photo, it is hard not to think of the prom in Derry. Jamie Penich decided to forgo that tradition for ten months of the sort of international life that Kenzi Snider thought of as everyday life.

CHAPTER 14

WHAT EVIDENCE DO YOU HAVE?

As Kenzi Snider lay on the bed in her off-campus apartment on February 4, 2002, writing out yet another account of the fatal St. Patrick's Day trip to Seoul, the three men investigating her huddled in a motel room across town.

Mansfield, Lee and DiVittis knew that with no forensic evidence, the only way to make a case against Kenzi was with a confession. The contradictions Mansfield had compiled might raise some eyebrows, but they were not nearly sufficient to file charges. Without her words, they had nothing.

The best way to win a confession, the investigators decided, was to use one of the most common interrogation techniques: minimization. Sometimes called face saving or theme development, detectives will present a suspect with a storyline that downplays his or her moral culpability for the crime in the hopes that the suspect will become comfortable enough to confess.

In a murder case, for example, officers may tell a suspect who denies everything that they know he is guilty, but believe he probably acted in self-defense or at the direction of an accomplice.

"No one typically walks into the room, meets with the police and just confesses to what they did. They need to be able to save face," Mansfield testified later.

It was a technique DiVittis used all the time.

"It's to change someone from denying to accepting [responsibility]," he recalled later. "You know [you tell suspects], 'It's not like you killed a hundred people. It's not that you planted a nuclear bomb.' So that their state of mind is 'I'm not a terrible person.'"

In Kenzi's case, the investigators decided the minimization storyline would be what the investigators began calling "the lesbian theme": the idea that Jamie's murder was the culmination of some sexual experimentation. Lee and Mansfield, bolstered by the profiler's assessment, believed this was a genuine possibility and, moreover, suggesting it might make Kenzi feel less blameworthy and more apt to confess.

The investigators began sowing the seeds of the lesbian theme at their first meeting when DiVittis said her dreams were a sign of sexual conflict. Lee had worked a related angle by downplaying the actual consequences of guilt. This area is a trickier corollary of minimizing moral culpability. Few detectives will actually tell a suspect that he will not go to prison if he confesses to murder, but investigators will hint at lighter sentences or other considerations.

Lee very consciously did this when he told her that if Jamie's killer was a foreigner, extradition might not be possible, and even if it was, the culprit would be treated like the soldier who got a short sentence for killing the prostitute.

The three investigators went over their strategy several times, reviewed some books of crime scene photos and then repaired to their rooms for the night. In Huntington, Kenzi was still up. Writing out everything she remembered about that weekend in Seoul took longer than she had anticipated, and by the time she finished the eighth and final page, it was 2 A.M.

The next afternoon, Kenzi was fifteen minutes early to the meeting at the Ramada. She came with two gifts for the investigators: her homework assignment and eight tubs of Italian gelato from an ice cream parlor near campus.

"They had asked me to come help as a friend, and I had not felt threatened by them in any way. So I thought that they . . . would enjoy ice cream," she recalled later.

For the agents, the tubs of chocolate and vanilla left little doubt that they had gained Kenzi's trust.

The four returned to Room 226. The mood was "light" and Kenzi "jovial," Mansfield later recalled. She sat down on the bed and told them that she was a little tired. She had gotten up at 6 that morning for her shift at the Barboursville School. The agents were sympathetic. Lee and DiVittis chatted with her about Huntington and her classes while Mansfield sat alone on top of a low bureau, reading over the new statement.

It was by far the most detailed account.

"March 17, 2001, Seoul, Korea. As a group, near 6 o'clock, after spending the morning touring Seoul, we all went to an Indian restaurant approximately two blocks from the Kum Sung Motel," she began.

Mansfield scoured the squiggly cursive for anything new or contradictory.

"Earlier in the evening, Jamie and I had been discussing how you could tell an American out of a crowd by their 'baseball butts.' We talked about this with the [hashers] and they had us compare all their butts and see which ones had 'baseball butts,'" she wrote.

That was new, but hardly important.

About Vince, she wrote, "He started telling me that if I would stay the night with him, he would pay for me to go to Jeju [Island] with him at the end of the month. I asked what I would have to do if I stayed the night. He said, 'Nothing, we could just lie next to each other or talk.' He said this as leaning in for a kiss. I turned away and said, 'No,' and he turned to block the way for me to go by as I started to stand up, so I stood on the table and stepped out."

That's consistent with her embellishing, Mansfield thought.

It wasn't until the very last page that Mansfield saw anything he thought was truly significant. Kenzi detailed going back to Room 103 to check on Jamie.

"I knocked lightly and asked if she's okay. I got no response so I opened the door and listened to the bathroom door. She sounded fine, all I heard was the shower. I closed the door and walked back to my room. I did not lock it," she wrote.

In her previous statement, she said she talked to

Jamie, but never opened the door. Now she was saying she opened the door but never talked to Jamie. She still doesn't have her story straight, Mansfield thought.

He looked up from the looseleaf sheet toward the bed, where Kenzi sat talking to Lee and DiVittis. He decided to hold off on confronting her.

Okay, Mansfield said. Let's just go through this one last time. Start from the moment you arrived in Korea and take us up through finding Jamie's body.

Kenzi nodded and began. As she talked about her classes at Keimyung and the dorm dynamics, Mansfield watched her carefully. Her bright blue eyes flashed from one agent to another. She smiled easily. She answered every question without hesitation. She was always upbeat. She struck him as eminently likable and intelligent. This woman is not like any suspect I have ever encountered, Mansfield thought.

"She seemed very comfortable speaking with us, and I was impressed with the way she carried herself. Very confident, but not overbearing," he recalled later.

For two and a half hours, Kenzi talked. Sitting on the bed, she recounted going to Seoul and renting a room in the Kum Sung and partying at Nickleby's and talking to the soldiers. Occasionally, Lee or Mansfield would toss her a question, but mostly she just narrated the trip.

The agents from Korea knew the story well, but this was the first time they had heard it directly from her. When she got to the part about checking on Jamie, she echoed what she had written in the homework assignment—she had opened the door to Room 103, heard the shower and assumed Jamie was fine.

As it began to grow dark outside, Mansfield felt

like he had heard enough. Sometime after 5 P.M., he took out the list of contradictions he had made months before, pushed himself up off the bureau and looked Kenzi in the eye.

We have some problems with what you are telling us, Kenzi, he said. His voice was cold and direct.

Vince says he never saw you on Hooker Hill. We've asked him and his friend and they are sure they never saw you, Mansfield added.

Everything else he's told us has checked out. So I guess I don't see why he would lie about seeing you, he continued.

Is he lying? Or are you? he asked.

The question took Kenzi aback.

I definitely saw him. We waved to each other, she replied.

He says he didn't, Mansfield said.

Maybe he had too much to drink. I don't really know . . . Kenzi said, her voice trailing off. Mansfield quickly moved on.

What about this homework you did for us? Now you say that you actually opened Jamie's door when you went back. You never said that in any of the five previous interviews you did, he told her.

I didn't even remember that until this summer, she told him. I kept thinking about it and finally I remembered exactly what happened. I told my mom, she added.

The investigators stared back at her.

Maybe I was struggling with guilt over not locking Jamie's door when I left. I just don't know, she said.

Mansfield pulled a crime scene photo from a binder. It showed the pile of Jamie's clothes on the bathroom floor. He pointed to the jeans, the underpants inside them and the bra beneath them.

Kenzi, he said, do you see something here that doesn't match your story?

She looked intently at the photo. After a pause, she asked, How is it that when I left her she was in her bra and underwear, but here her underwear is inside her jeans?

We thought maybe you could tell us that, Mansfield said.

I don't know, she said.

Mansfield continued down his list of contradictions for nearly an hour "just [long] enough to find out that Miss Snider couldn't answer the questions, could not satisfy the problem that we had there," he later recalled.

As the agents had planned, DiVittis took over the interview. He rose from a chair, crossed the motel room and sat down next to Kenzi on the bed.

He "began to tell her that everything in the statements, everything that we had uncovered up to that point was showing us clearly that she had killed Miss Penich," Mansfield later testified.

Kenzi "listened for approximately five or ten minutes. It seemed like a long time before [she] said anything," Mansfield later recalled.

Finally, she spoke.

"You're saying that I killed Jamie," she said.

"Yes," DiVittis replied. "That is exactly what we are saying."

She stood up, dropped her jaw and stared at the agents. Suddenly, she and DiVittis were talking over each other.

"What evidence do you have?"

"We don't think you meant to do it."

"Are you trying to scare me?"

"Sometimes, you'll hide a memory and cover it up with another one that you can handle."

"Those words don't mean anything to me."

"Let's just talk this out."

"Do I need a lawyer?"

"That would complicate things."

Kenzi put up her hand and turned to Mansfield.

"I have to leave the room. I'll be right back. I promise I'll be right back. Can I just leave the room for a minute?" she asked.

Mansfield was stunned.

"That's fine," he heard himself say.

She walked past Lee and DiVittis. The door slammed shut behind her.

The agents stared at one another in panic. They had come all this way, and as things stood, they had nothing. No confession, not even an incriminating statement, and she was well within her rights to walk to the elevator and leave the motel.

Ten seconds passed, and then there was a knock on the door. Kenzi stood in the threshold. "You knew this when you talked to me yesterday," she said to Mansfield.

Come in and talk to us, Kenzi, DiVittis told her.

"If I did this, I don't remember doing it," she said as she walked back into the room.

DiVittis grabbed an easy chair from the corner of the room and slid it so that it was facing the window with the view of the trees and the parking lot. He told her to sit down, and he stood against the window directly in front of her.

Let's give him room to work, Lee said to Mansfield.

They walked to the far side of the room and stood in the foyer by the bathroom where they could hear Kenzi, but she could not see them.

It was 6:30 P.M.

Over the next five hours, in stops and starts, Kenzi confessed to murdering Jamie.

CHAPTER 15

A WONDERFUL HUMAN BEING

Hunched over in the easy chair, her body shaking and her eyes clenched shut, Kenzi Snider finally uttered the words the investigators longed to hear.

"I killed her!" she cried out.

For a moment, her whimpers were the only sounds in the motel room. DiVittis, standing directly in front of her with his back against the window, stared down at her. Tears dripped from her face and into her lap. Mansfield, taking notes from a spot behind the chair, and Lee, who stood near the door, locked eyes. *Could this really be happening?* they seemed to ask each other.

The clock on the night stand read 8:30. It had been

two hours since DiVittis directed Kenzi to the easy chair and took charge of the questioning.

We know you did this, he had told her then. It's just a matter of helping you figure out what happened.

Kenzi shook her head.

"If I killed her, I don't remember it," she told him.

An experienced interrogator, DiVittis heard in her answer an opening for the minimization technique. "*If I killed her*"? Why not a simple "I didn't kill her"?

He began talking to her about traumatic memories and how good people who did something totally out of character could cover up the event with other memories.

She looked at him quizzically.

Maybe it's just too tough to remember, he suggested. His comments became what he later termed a monologue.

"You let them know you know what happened, and it's futile for them to continue denying what happened," he said afterward.

He talked about the possible effects of alcohol. He raised the lesbian angle. Maybe you were turned on by Jamie. We need to figure out what triggered this, he told her.

"There are a lot of things that happen to people that cause them to do things they never think they would ever do," he told her.

Do you want us to help you figure this out or not? It's up to you, he said.

I do want to know what happened, she told him.

Okay, he said, let's go back to that night.

Watching from across the hotel room, Lee was

amazed. He had never seen a murder interrogation before and was astonished by DiVittis's skill. *My job,* he told himself, *is just to stand here like a tree trunk and let the professional work.*

DiVittis's questions gradually became more intense and confrontational. Kenzi became more emotional and hesitant about her answers.

Lee felt the hairs on the back of his neck stand on end.

"She did it," he thought. "She did it and she's going to confess."

The confession came haltingly and through sobs, but it boiled down to this: Kenzi admitted killing Jamie during a lesbian encounter after they returned to the motel. Her answers to DiVittis's questions did not always make sense, and both he and Kenzi jumped around in the chronology. Mansfield realized he should make some sort of record of the interview and grabbed a stack of copier paper and a pen and began scribbling down what Kenzi said as fast as he could. A barebones narrative began to emerge:

Kenzi and Jamie returned from the Kum Sung after several hours at Nickleby's. They went to Room 103. Jamie immediately came on to Kenzi in the bathroom. They began kissing and stroking each other.

"I touched her chest and back," Mansfield quoted Kenzi as saying.

Kenzi performed oral sex on Jamie. Jamie then tried to undo Kenzi's pants. As Jamie reached for her waistband, Kenzi flashed back to an unpleasant incident when she was four and her brothers and some other boys tried to look up her skirt. Kenzi became enraged with Jamie.

"I don't want her touching my button!!" Mansfield quoted her. He added, "Deep sobbing."

Kenzi backhanded Jamie across the face, knocking her into the bathtub. Jamie slumped uncomfortably in the tub.

"I did not go for help because I didn't want anyone to know," Mansfield quoted Kenzi.

Kenzi lifted Jamie up and tried to carry her into the bedroom. She tripped over a ledge leading into the room and dropped Jamie against the wall. She picked her up again and laid her on her back. She thought Jamie was staring up at her, and that made her angry again. She stomped on her head and chest.

"I feel my foot, and it's heavy. I see her chest. My foot is heavy. Pushing she's pushing on foot. She knows what I'm doing. I push harder, her chest," Mansfield scrawled out.

Repulsed by what she had done, she covered Jamie's head with the jacket, returned to her room, locked the door and crawled over Jeroen and into bed.

As she gave the account, Kenzi told DiVittis again and again that the memories were just coming to her. She had been repressing them for a year, and now images from that night were flooding back, she said. When Mansfield flipped through a book of crime scene photos, she stopped him on a shot of a bloody footprint in the foyer. "That's mine," she said. How can you be sure? he asked, adding, "Most people don't look at the bottom of their shoes." She replied, "It's mine."

Although DiVittis reassured her that repressing these traumatic memories was normal, neither he nor the other two agents actually believed it. It's a common effort for criminals to save face, they thought.

"I personally didn't believe that a person could forget doing something like that. So to me it's evasive," Mansfield said later. It reminded him of so many soldiers who had told him they were too drunk to remember their roles in bar fights.

It was just a story she was telling to make herself appear less evil, the investigators felt. It was easier to say she'd buried the memory than to admit that she'd spent a year lying to Jamie's family and her own relatives and friends.

Just before midnight, the agents asked if she would let them search her off-campus apartment. They were looking for the clothing and boots she had worn that night and any journals she had kept. She escorted them to the apartment and pointed out jeans and a plaid shirt. The items matched the outfit Kenzi was wearing in the photos the hashers took at Nickleby's. Mansfield held them up to his nose, and they smelled of laundry softener. It had been a year since the murder, and Kenzi said she had worn and washed the shirt and pants many times. He did not see any stains on the pants, but put them in an evidence bag for testing at an army crime lab in Georgia.

What they didn't find was the boots. Kenzi told them she did not know where they were. They were a cheap generic brand, and the last time she had seen them was in Minnesota. She had either put them in storage there or thrown them away. Lee arranged for FBI agents in St. Cloud to search for the boots.

As he wandered through Kenzi's apartment, Lee was still trying to digest her confession.

"It was an amazing, amazing experience. It was like poetry," he later said.

He looked at the young blond woman helping Mansfield find things in her apartment. It was just a campus efficiency, but she had decorated it with care. The art and photos and keepsakes reflected her international travels. Lee paged through her scrapbooks and journals as the other agents talked. They included letters from pen pals around the world, Girl Scout badges, report cards and photos of all the places she had lived.

"She seemed to know exactly what she wanted and was a good student and [did] volunteer activities," he recalled.

"She's a wonderful human being," he concluded.

It was this fundamental goodness that led her to confess, he later said, "to unburden herself from that cancerous knowledge."

The mood in Kenzi's apartment was markedly different from the tense atmosphere during her confession.

"They kept assuring me that I was still a good person and it's not my fault, that things happen, we don't hate you, now you can get your life back, now you can go on," Kenzi recalled later. They told her they would have a few more questions in the morning, and then they left her alone.

Back at the Ramada, Lee placed a phone call to an official at the embassy. The man was not in his office, but Lee insisted his secretary track him down. When he finally came to the phone, the official was irritated.

"You just interrupted a meeting with a four-star general. This better be good," he told the FBI agent.

"I think you'll be happy," Lee told him. "We just got a full confession to Jamie Penich's murder. It's over."

"Great news, great, great news," the official replied.

The next day, Kenzi drove herself out to the motel. As she and Mansfield waited for the elevator up to the room, he asked her how she felt.

"She said that she had slept well, better than she had in a very long time, and that she was remembering a lot more," he said later.

Back in the room, they asked her to dictate a confession to Mansfield. He did not have a tape recorder or a computer, so he had to write it out long hand.

> We were arm and arm walking home. We got into the room. [Jamie] unbuttoned my plaid shirt and drops [it] in the corner. She checks on Anna and says we have to be quiet. She takes my hand we walk into the bathroom. I don't know who turned on the light. She's by the tub. She takes off [my] bra. She takes off her bra, jeans and underwear. She takes my hand, pulls me closer and we start to kiss. I don't know how long we're kissing. I start playing with her chest. I kissed her down her stomach. She's still standing and I go to kiss down there. I don't know how long. We kiss a bit more. She kinda pushed me back. She moves her arms around me and is playing with my waist. She's going for my button. I move away. I'm thinking no, but I can't get it to come out. She goes for my button again. I hit her hard. She's in the bathtub. She looks hurt. She's quiet. She hit her head. She looks uncomfortable. I don't mean to hit her, but I'm mad at her. I'm angry. I go to pick her up. She's heavy. I trip and she falls. Her head hits the

floor. We're outside. I trip on the thing in the floor. I'm mad at her. She's still unconscious. I pick her up and move her again. She doesn't make me feel any better. I am hurt and I am angry. I don't want her looking at me. She won't stop looking at me. I don't know why, and I pick up my foot and it's heavy. I don't know how many times I hit her. I don't know how many times. And then I just stare at her. I don't know, but I pick up a jacket. I didn't know it was a jacket, and cover her head and she's not looking anymore. And I stare. I don't know but I pick up my shirt and I go and lock everything out. I didn't mean to.

Mansfield felt there were still some problems with her confession. She had never explained the blood-soaked rag found near Jamie's body or mentioned the tooth that had been knocked across the room. Additionally, she did not explain the drop of saliva on Jamie's chest. Kissing her there might have left some saliva, but not the amount the Korean police described. Mansfield and Lee, however, were wary of pushing too hard for more details.

"We were worried about the damage to her mental stability," Lee said. The follow-up questions Mansfield asked were gentle:

Q: Where are you standing while you're using [*your*] foot?

A: I'm above her. I'm above Jamie. Anna is behind me.

Q: The item you discussed stepping on, where is it?

A: I think it's what I used to cover her face. It's beside the right side of her face. When I'm standing and staring at her I have to reach over her, to her right side to pick it up.

Q: You had described last night that Jamie used her hands to push on your foot. Is this true?

A: My foot was heavy. Last night was hazy. This isn't hazy.

Q: When you dropped Jamie, where did she land exactly?

A: At the bathroom door. I trip on the ledge. I see her in the corner. Her head's in the corner. It's tilted up in the corner.

Q: What corner?

A: The corner of the ledge in the room. Her toes are in the bathroom door. She's crooked. My back is against the wall. Her head is to the left of me. Her arm's on my shoes.

Q: Her tooth is found in that corner. Did she fall face down?

A: I don't know. I don't know.

Q: Last night you described wiping your shoes. What did you do?

A: I don't remember. I don't know. I stepped on the thing above her head.

Q: How are you feeling right now?

A: I didn't mean too! [*sic*]

Q: Did you have a relationship with Jamie before that night?

A: No, we were just friends. I didn't know she or I felt that way.

Q: Did you believe Jamie was dead when you left the room?

A: I just stare[d]. I knew she was pretty and couldn't look like that.

Q: When you left the room did you know you killed Jamie?

A: I don't know. I am staring. I'm not angry anymore. She doesn't make me feel angry anymore.

Q: When did the bathroom light go off?

A: I don't know. It's off, maybe I bump it. I don't know.

Q: Do you remember paper under your feet?

A: I don't hear noises now. It's dark, it's dark. I can't hear noises.

Q: Did you kill Jamie?

A: Yes, I didn't mean to. I was angry. She kept looking at me. I don't know. I was angry. I didn't want her touching my button. I killed her.

Q: Is there anything to add?

A: I don't remember the rag or the tooth.

Later that day, Kenzi agreed to let local FBI agents fingerprint and photograph her. They did not arrest her, however. A warrant could be issued only by authorities in Korea, where the crime had occurred.

Before they left, Lee and Mansfield met one last time with Kenzi. It was a cordial meeting. The agents gave her a Snickers bar and thanked her for "helping everyone get their lives back," she remembered later. They instructed her not to tell anyone of her confession and to check with them before leaving the state. As Lee later described it, the conversation had the tone of parents talking with a worried child.

"We felt almost protective of her," he recalled. He slowly explained that he had to return to Korea to talk to the authorities there, and the process might take a while.

"Hang in there, though," he told her.

Kenzi asked if she could still become a teacher. "Of course," she remembered them saying. Then they left her alone.

CHAPTER 16

OF COURSE IT'S HER

"**Y**ou just let her go?"

The FBI supervisor was incredulous. On February 6, 2002, on their way out of Huntington, Lee placed a courtesy call to the head of the FBI in Pittsburgh, the office responsible for bureau activities in the region.

Let me get this straight, the man barked at them. You got a confession out of her and then you just drove away and left her there?

It sounded bad, Lee conceded, but they had no choice. The murder of Jamie Penich had occurred on Korean soil. Neither the FBI nor the U.S. Army had any jurisdiction. Only prosecutors in Seoul could make out an arrest warrant, and they didn't even know about the confession yet.

Lee and Mansfield hurried back to Korea, armed with Kenzi's confession. The Korean detectives were stunned.

"I think they were embarrassed. We didn't emphasize that. We never said, 'Oh, if only you guys would've taken an impression of her boots.' No, we never said anything like that," he recalled.

The Koreans were impressed with Lee's description of the confession, but drawing up an arrest warrant proved a complicated process. Korean prosecutors required translations of Mansfield's reports, his handwritten notes from the initial confession, Kenzi's homework assignment and her dictated final confession. Then the prosecutors wrote a long summary to show to a judge. Lee had envisioned it taking a day or two to get the paperwork in order, but the days stretched into weeks.

Back in Huntington, Kenzi tried to resume her normal life at Marshall. She took her regular shifts at the Barboursville School and attended her classes. To her friends, however, it was obvious that something was wrong. She cried often and seemed distracted. What's wrong with you? they asked. Kenzi remembered the agents' admonition against talking about what had happened in the Ramada. She just shook her head. I can't talk about it, she said.

A boy she'd started dating before the agents came to town, a Marshall student who wanted to someday run for governor, told her she could trust him, but she remembered his political ambitions and thought, "He'll run away from me the moment he hears."

After a few days, she stopped going to classes. She told Janet Dozier, her early education professor, that "she was going through some things and she wasn't sure if she was going to continue with school or not." The professor was confused. Kenzi was one of her best students.

Do you want to switch to an independent study? she asked.

Kenzi brushed off the suggestion.

"She said she just didn't feel like she could focus," Dozier remembered.

Kenzi phoned Clark Egnor, the international studies administrator who had helped her get involved with the ESL teacher training as a way to get her mind off the murder. If I have to drop out of school for a little while, will I lose my spot in the program? he remembered her asking.

"I told her I couldn't make any guarantees," he recalled. "I got the impression that there was some very significant personal reason why she needed to drop out, but I didn't explore it, I didn't feel like it was my business."

On February 11, 2002, five days after Lee, Mansfield and DiVittis had left town, Kenzi formally withdrew from Marshall. She stayed in Huntington, working at the school for troubled teens and visiting friends. She was not the upbeat girl they knew. She often sat in their dorm rooms or apartments staring off into space.

During this time, she never consulted a lawyer or a therapist. She did not call her brothers, then living in Minnesota and Rhode Island, or confide in her mother, who was still teaching in Thailand.

Once she reached out to her father, who was living in Florida. The two had never been close, and since the divorce, she had only sporadic contact with him. She phoned him after she dropped out of college and asked if she could stay with him.

"She said something really upsetting had happened and she just couldn't deal with school anymore," Roger Snider recalled. Probably boy trouble, he thought.

"I told her that we could work something out, but she didn't call back," he said. "It was two weeks later that I heard that she was arrested."

On February 28, 2002, FBI agents tracked Kenzi down at a friend's apartment in Huntington and placed her in handcuffs. They read her a translation of an arrest warrant signed the day before by Judge Chin-Su Chung of the Seoul District Court: Kenzi Noris Elizabeth Snider is wanted for the murder of Jamie Lynn Penich, a crime punishable by a sentence of death by hanging.

The agents drove her to the federal courthouse and placed her in a holding cell. She was allowed one phone call. Many young women who find themselves in jail for the first time might have used the opportunity to call their parents or a lawyer. Kenzi phoned the Barboursville School to tell them that she would miss her next shift.

"My family would find out, and it wasn't like I was going anywhere, but [her supervisors at the school] needed to know so they could get someone else to work," she explained.

The next morning, two of the FBI agents who had arrested her came into her cell with more questions. During the interview at the Ramada, she was never in formal custody and therefore did not require a Miranda warning, but in federal lockup, she was in police custody, and the agents told her she had the right to remain silent and the right to a lawyer.

She shook her head and signed a waiver form.

"I asked Miss Snider to give me a statement covering the points that she had given during her previous confession to the Army criminal investigative agent and the two FBI agents here in Huntington," agent Linwood Smith later testified.

Kenzi immediately launched into a statement that began with her arrival in Korea for the study-abroad program. She walked Smith and his partner through the trip to Seoul and the night at Nickleby's.

The agent was struck by her nonchalant demeanor.

"It would be just like talking about a football game or the weather or anything else," he said.

But when Kenzi arrived at the point in her account when she and Jamie entered Room 103, she started to hesitate.

She paused and said, "This is the hard part."

"We looked at her and asked for an explanation, 'What happened? What do you mean?'" Smith testified.

"And she said that at that point it was hard for her to distinguish between what she actually remembered doing in the room with Miss Penich and what she had heard from other sources that had happened in the room to Miss Penich," the agent said.

Eventually, however, Kenzi continued the account. In his report, Smith documented another confession:

> Snider "went down on" Penich who eventually brought Snider's head up and reached down to Snider's waist. When Penich touched Snider's pants button, Snider "stopped thinking." Snider became so angry that she could not speak and says she was not rational. Snider hit Penich with her hand ... Penich hit her head on the tub and became unresponsive. Snider stared at Penich, who "looked uncomfortable" in the bathroom floor. Snider tried to lift Penich up and move her out of the bathroom but tripped and fell into the wall, dropping Penich in the process. Snider again tried to straighten Penich out, but then noticed that Penich seemed to be looking at her. Snider reacted emotionally and "made [Penich] stop looking at me with my foot." Snider cannot remember how many times she stomped on Penich. After Snider stopped, she picked up something (Snider was told later it was Penich's jacket) and put it over Penich's face. Snider then picked up her shirt and returned to her own room. When asked what she told the Korean police during the initial interview, Snider said she did not remember what happened until after she had spoken with the police.

In Derry that winter, as investigators zeroed in on Kenzi, the Penichs remained under the impression that a serviceman had killed their daughter. They trudged through every day thinking that very little or nothing was being done to bring the perpetrator to justice. No one from the CID or the embassy had told them about Mansfield's list of contradictions or the investigators' plan to come to the United States to question Kenzi, or the result of that interrogation. It was better to keep them in the dark than to raise their hopes falsely, the investigators felt.

At the end of February, with the arrest warrant wending its way toward Huntington, an FBI agent from Pittsburgh called and told them to expect a break in the case. The agent wouldn't say much, but Patty noted he kept referring to "someone" and "this person" and "the suspect" rather than the pronoun she expected: he. She was still puzzling over it on February 28 when the agent called back. Kenzi Snider has been charged with Jamie's murder, he said. She's in jail in West Virginia.

Brian and Patty were floored. Kenzi? But what about the military guys? they asked. We have a full confession, the agent told them. It's her. The Penichs could hardly grasp what he was saying. The girl they had talked to on the phone? The girl who had e-mailed with them? She did this? We were worried about her. Patty thought back on their discussions about Nick Baer. *We felt she might be in danger*, Patty thought.

After they got off the phone with the FBI, the Penichs stared at each other. They have a signed confession, they repeated. After all this, it's her. As the idea began to sink in, they went back over all their contact with Kenzi. Signs of guilt began to appear. Brian remembered a conversation with Jamie the week before the murder in which she told him that a girl named Kenzi was "mothering" her in an irritating way. And then there was all Kenzi's interest in the investigation. So many e-mails back and forth. None of the other exchange students had done that. And what about her close friendship with Jeff? At the time, it had seemed sort of sweet that they could comfort each other, but it now struck them as strange. Patty also remembered Kenzi's trip to the Netherlands to visit Anneloes right after the murder. *You know someone two weeks and you're going to fly all the way around the world to stay with them?* she thought. *Maybe she went to threaten Anneloes—or collude with her,* Patty thought. The signs were there and we just missed them, the Penichs told each other.

"In retrospect, it's like, of course, it's her," Patty said.

Kenzi had not phoned any relatives, but her brothers learned through reporters asking for comment. In Thailand, Kenzi's mother, Heath Bozonie, woke to a two-word e-mail from a family friend: "Call home."

When she reached her sons, they told her the stunning news. They have a confession, mom, they added. She booked a flight back to the United States and then curled up on her bed and cried. How could this be? She had been with Kenzi just days after the murder. Kenzi was so distraught, she thought. She tried to imagine a scenario in which her only daughter, whom she had never known to be violent, had killed a friend. All she could come up with was drugs. If someone had drugged her, "maybe her body could have done it but never her heart, never her mind, never her soul could have done this," she said.

In Huntington, her friends and professors read and

reread the short arrest notice in the local paper. It can't be true, they told one another. That is just not the woman we know.

In Daegu, Dr. Kim was reading the newspaper over a cup of coffee when she came across a story about Jamie's murder. *Kenzi*, she choked. *Is this possible?* She remembered the American girl in the police station. She had been so angry about her treatment by the detectives. And she had snapped at Dr. Kim when she found out other students were making calls home. *Was this all part of the act?* Dr. Kim thought. *Was the anger part of the cover-up?*

Thanks to the Internet, the story of Kenzi's arrest bounced from one exchange student to another in a matter of minutes. Some who had known Kenzi and Jamie in Daegu couldn't believe it.

"I was shocked and confused," Bakary Bakayoko, the head of the foreign students, said. He remembered Kenzi and Jamie walking around campus together and gossiping about boys. No, he said to himself, she could not have done it.

In Holland, Anneloes and her parents were dumbfounded. They had hosted Kenzi for three weeks after the murder and felt betrayed. We had a murderer in our house, eating our food, listening to our conversations, they thought. Anneloes contacted Jeroen Kuilman, who went online to read the stories himself.

"The idea that Kenzi could have done it never crossed my mind before, so it was hard to accept it as true," he recalled. "On the other hand, she had admitted it herself and told the story in such great detail that it simply had to be true."

He thought about that morning in the motel. Kenzi and he had raced into Room 103 side by side. Kenzi had seemed shocked by the scene.

"She must've been really good at acting to fake this, must have spent the whole night thinking about how to react or something or have some kind of split personality [because] her reaction was not different from that of others," he remembered.

Like the Penichs, he began to look back for warning signs he missed. He couldn't find anything, but wondered if her upbringing should have been a clue.

"She could never be friends with somebody very long, and it's therefore hard for a person in her position to get too attached to friends," he said later.

CHAPTER 17

ANOTHER COUNTRY TO NAVIGATE

The reports about the arrest hinted at a sexual motive, but it was not until weeks later, when the Koreans began filing paperwork, that the full, sensational details of Kenzi's confession became public. In a case summary, a Korean prosecutor outlined Kenzi's statements about the sexual contact leading to the murder.

> Penich motioned Snider to be quiet, putting her index finger to her lips, and took Snider to the bathroom by hand. Penich then took off her bra and "shimmied" out of her pants and panties in one motion. Penich then pulled Snider closer to her and they kissed . . . Snider and Penich kissed for an undetermined amount of time and at some

> point Snider touched and kissed Penich's geni-
> tals. This act also continued for an undetermined
> amount of time. Penich then pulled Snider up from
> her kneeling position and they kissed each other
> again. Penich gently pushed Snider away from
> her and touched Snider's pants button in order to
> remove her pants to return Snider's affection.
> Snider backed away from Penich, bumping into
> the toilet, but Penich again approached Snider
> and touched her pants button. Snider stated she
> wanted to tell Penich to stop but could not
> speak . . .

The Penichs were furious. In effect, Kenzi was painting Jamie as a would-be gay rapist or at the very least a
sexual aggressor who had brought on her own death.
Not only had Kenzi taken their daughter's life, they
thought, but she's trying to take her reputation too. Jamie was not gay, her parents said.

It didn't even make sense, Patty thought. Jamie was
five inches shorter and eighty pounds lighter than
Kenzi.

"Kenzi is an Amazon compared to Jamie," Patty
Penich said. If someone was going to be pushed
around, it certainly wouldn't be Kenzi, Patty thought.

"I think Kenzi wanted Jamie sexually, and when Jamie told her to bug off or a little bit angrier words than
that, she got angry and she pushed her," she said.

While everyone she knew reacted to the news that
she was a murderer, Kenzi sat alone in the holding cell

in Huntington. She would later say that she thought about her confession for hours on end.

"I wasn't thinking so much I'm a murderer, I was more along the lines of I just signed my name to saying I killed my friend," she recalled.

I told them that I hooked up with Jamie, killed her and then repressed the whole thing for a year, she remembered thinking. *I talked to Jamie's dad the day of her funeral, and I never realized that I was the reason for the funeral. I spoke to Jeff Gretz for hours, and I never got that he was heartbroken because of me. That is what I told them.*

The problem, she would say later, was that she had two competing sets of memories. She remembered kissing Jamie and then stomping on her neck with her boot. But she still had the other memories too. She could see Jamie standing by the shower in her underpants and bra. She could hear herself saying good night. She could remember walking back to her room. Which of these memories was right? The one where she killed Jamie? Or the one where she left her alive?

She would later say that for long periods of time in jail, she ran through each account and tried to focus only on the things she was absolutely positive had occurred. She said that she kept coming back to two things: Vince and the faucet. She remembered the way Vince looked as he walked up the alley. She could see his crew cut and his muscles and Martinez standing beside him. And she could remember the way the shower faucet felt in her hand, how she turned it to adjust the water and the sound of the drops splattering on the tub.

"Everything else I was able to be told I was lying about . . . and able to believe that my memories of dropping Jamie off were unreal," she said. *But not those two things. Those, I know for sure,* she thought.

In the Ramada, Seung Lee had told Kenzi that extraditing an American to Korea was difficult, if not impossible. In fact, it had never been done. The extradition treaty between the two countries went into effect in 1999 and had yet to be tested. If extradited, Kenzi would be the first American citizen sent to Korea to face charges.

The process set out in the treaty was not very complicated. The Korean government sent a binder of evidence to the U.S. State Department, which handed off the information to federal prosecutors in West Virginia. It was up to the assistant U.S. attorneys there to convince a federal magistrate that there was probable cause to believe Kenzi was the killer. That standard, much lower than the proof beyond a reasonable doubt required at trial, meant the federal prosecutors had to show only enough evidence to establish that there was a fair probability Kenzi Snider killed Jamie Penich. If they could do that, she would be on a plane to face trial in Korea.

The day after her arrest, Kenzi filled out a form to get a free lawyer. She wrote that she earned $700 a month at the Barboursville School, had $900 in a savings account and received a $1,500 annual federal college grant. She owed $575 every month for rent and utilities, and she had run up a $2,200 debt on her credit card.

The court deemed her indigent and gave her a federal public defender from Charleston, Edward Weis. At their first meeting, Weis gave his young client a fairly standard warning: Don't talk about your case to anyone other than me. Kenzi nodded. I mean it, he said. Not your cellmate, not your parents, not your friends. For the rest of her time in West Virginia, she never talked about the murder or the confession unless Weis was with her.

A diminutive, bespectacled Philadelphia native, Weis was an experienced and well-respected attorney who knew his way around every courtroom and type of case in the Southern District of West Virginia. But like his opponents, the prosecutors, and the magistrate, he was completely unfamiliar with extradition cases. Federal court in West Virginia meant crystal meth, cocaine, guns and the occasional bank robbery. In a jurisdiction where people had closer ties to other countries, extraditions would have been relatively routine, but only 1 percent of West Virginians are foreign-born. No one involved in the case remembered an extradition in the state.

That spring, as Kenzi was moved from federal lockup in Huntington to a regional jail in Charleston, the lawyers were pulling dusty case books down from their shelves.

For Weis, the first order of business was to get Kenzi out on bail while he and his opponents figured out the extradition process. The magistrate, Maurice Taylor, agreed to hold a bail hearing March 11, 2002, just two weeks after Kenzi's arrest. For tiny Huntington, the proceeding was big news. A handful of TV trucks parked in front of the Sidney L. Christie Federal Building on

Fifth Street, and newspaper reporters from Huntington, Charleston and Pittsburgh were also on hand. The last proceeding to attract any kind of outside attention had been the murder trials of some bank robbers in the 1980s.

Because of the interest, court officials moved the hearing from Taylor's small courtroom to a larger, ornate courtroom on the second floor. Just before the proceeding began, U.S. marshals escorted Kenzi down the aisle of the courtroom. She was dressed in a Day-Glo orange jumpsuit and wore ankle shackles and handcuffs. The marshals had instructed her to face forward in the courtroom and not to communicate in any way with the people in the spectators' gallery. As she shuffled down the aisle, she glimpsed her mother, father and brothers, and rows and rows of Marshall classmates.

After the magistrate took the bench, Weis called two of Kenzi's friends as character witnesses.

"She is very selfless. She would show up and bring me breakfast at work, leave a flower on my door with a note that just says what a great friend . . . I am to her," a Marshall senior named Carmen Dillon testified.

"When was the last time she left a flower on your door?" Weiss asked Dillon.

"The day she was arrested," she replied.

Another Marshall student and a coworker at the Barboursville School told the magistrate he had never noticed any violent tendencies in Kenzi, especially not when she was drunk.

"She is actually a very nice drunk. She is very loving and caring," Eugene Johnson said. Weis entered Kenzi's dean's list certificate and her most recent report card into evidence. Janet Dozier, Kenzi's early education professor, also took the witness stand and told the magistrate that she was willing to let Kenzi live with her family if she was released on bail.

Weis told the magistrate the Snider family collectively could put up about $30,000 to secure her bond.

The federal prosecutors objected strenuously.

The "case for bond consists of a few college friends who know her primarily on campus and who have known her for a very short time and in very limited circumstances. There is nothing from her family. There is nothing from anyone who has known her for a very long period of time," assistant U.S. attorney Larry Ellis told the judge.

"She is something of an itinerant," he added.

Magistrate Taylor agreed. She was a flight risk, he said. Her ties to the community were tenuous and the charge against her was the most serious imaginable: capital murder. No bail, he ruled.

The hearing had lasted only forty-five minutes.

The marshals quickly ushered out Kenzi. Her mother and brothers drove to the jail to visit her, but her father left town immediately. He had not seen his ex-wife since the divorce and felt like an outsider at the family gathering.

"It was just uncomfortable all around. I wasn't really a part of it. Her mother was handling everything," he said later.

That evening in the jail in Charleston, Kenzi and her family were permitted to meet in a visiting room. Before long, uproarious giggling and happy voices echoed down the hall, puzzling guards. Inside, the Sniders were laughing about the orange jumpsuit, the jail food, the way the lawyers talked in court, anything that came to mind. Despite the dire circumstances, the Sniders were upbeat. This was their strong suit, after all: being resilient in strange, uncomfortable new situations. Capital murder charges would just be another country they had to learn to navigate. The Charleston jail would just be another adventure that they would laugh about later. Just make the best of it, they seemed to say with each chuckle.

On her own, Kenzi was no different. She quickly befriended her cellmate, a woman also accused of murder. Every day she wrote hopeful letters to friends and relatives. The jail did not allow paints, so Kenzi crushed M&M's shells and used them to make watercolors. She painted birds and rainbows on paper and sent them to her friends.

Did you hear about Kenzi and the M&M's? they said to one another when they passed on campus. She is incredible, they told one another.

When she received an encouraging note from a stranger, a teacher at a Christian school who felt it was her mission to write to prisoners, Kenzi dutifully wrote back. She and the woman quickly became dedicated pen pals, and soon the teacher and her son were driving four hours each way to visit her. It was just another friend in another odd situation.

She began tutoring other inmates in a GED program and started a Bible study with other inmates. She wrote to the teacher, "Why we hadn't earlier is beyond me and I presume Satan was loving every minute of it, but God won!"

Her letters were unfailingly positive.

"I consider it a great blessing to have come to jail. My walk with God has increased by countless measures," she wrote.

After she was denied bail, Kenzi met with Weis, and they began talking about the facts of the case. She told him that she was confused as to whether she had killed Jamie. I know I confessed to it, she said, but I have this other set of memories too. She told him she was certain she had seen Vincent on the street and had turned on the shower in Room 103. When I was arrested, she said, I only felt about 50 percent sure I committed murder, and the more time I have to think about it in jail, the more doubts I have. As a veteran defense attorney, Weis certainly would have been skeptical. He was used to defendants trying to backpedal from incriminating statements to the police. Kenzi seemed different though. She was not accusing investigators of making up a confession or tricking her into giving one. She was painting herself as utterly confused by her own words.

Weis began poring over the evidence file that the federal prosecutors had turned over to him. He reviewed the forensic reports and the statements of the students, the soldiers, the motel manager and his wife and Miss Yi.

When he was done, he picked up his phone and dialed a number in California.

"I think I've got a case for you," he began.

CHAPTER 18

SEEING PICTURES

Richard Ofshe is an emeritus professor in Berkeley's sociology department, but he has little use for the classroom or the lab. His passion lies in jail cells, witness boxes and, if all goes well, a television news magazine. Ofshe is the country's leading expert in false confessions by criminal suspects, an academic area increasingly familiar to the general public thanks to a handful of high-profile exonerations, including those on Illinois's death row and in the Central Park jogger case.

He has worked on many of the biggest cases as an expert witness and frequently lectures to conventions of judges and defense attorneys on how to spot a false confession. He contends that while coerced confessions by police are rare in the United States, "there is no doubt they occur regularly."

He is a controversial figure, lauded by the defense bar, loathed in law enforcement circles and scoffed at by the academic elite.

"My colleagues think what I do is bullshit," he says unapologetically. "Too real world."

Prosecutors and police detectives believe he exaggerates the frequency of false confessions. They also feel the police techniques he blames for coerced confessions are actually smart strategies good investigators use every day to get guilty people to admit to their crimes. Law enforcement associations have compiled a dossier of attack questions to help prosecutors undermine his testimony as an expert witness.

Ofshe's lifestyle and personality also put him at odds with his law and order opponents. He works for arguably the most liberal university in the country and lives with his wife in a large home filled with modern art and antiques on a hill high above Berkeley. The couple also maintains residences in the Caribbean and Paris. When he is in California, Ofshe spends most of his days in his plush home office with Lulu, a coton de tulear from a special breeder in France, sleeping in a white ball by his loafers.

By Ofshe's own description, he is egotistical and abrasive. On the witness stand, he can come off as superior and spoiling for a fight. Indeed, he loves confrontation and always relishes the opportunity to grill police about their interrogation methods.

"It's a great moment when that happens," he says. "They are full of shit, and they know they are full of shit."

Ofshe was born and raised in Queens, and he says the anger he brings to his work is part of a "New York Jew attitude."

"It's an ethnic thing, a reaction to the needless injustice," he says.

Ofshe is an admitted media hound. He has a small tape library of his television appearances, and his office is decorated with expensively framed articles about him. He points out his favorite two to visitors, one from the *New Yorker* and the other from the *New York Times Magazine*.

"For a boy from Fresh Meadows, it doesn't get any better than this," he says, before cuing up a tape of an appearance on *Dateline*.

Ofshe's willingness to cooperate with the press—and in some cases, to actually pitch stories to reporters—has made him well-known among defense lawyers.

"If a lawyer has a potential false confession and he can't find me after 20 minutes of looking, it's a prima facie case of incompetence," he says, only half joking.

Ofshe says that on average, he gets a phone call every day from a lawyer with a client who is claiming he or she falsely confessed. He turns down more than half the cases, he says, because there is no evidence of coercion, and he suspects the client is simply lying.

In the spring of 2002, however, the call from West Virginia sparked his interest. The only real evidence in the murder case is Kenzi Snider's confession, Weis told him. There are no forensics and no eyewitnesses, and in fact there was ample evidence pointing to a male culprit. There also may have been some influence by a powerful U.S. senator, the public defender told him.

Intrigued, Ofshe told him to run down the case.

Weis gave him a barebones account of the murder. He then told him about the motel manager's wife with her account of a Caucasian man with bloody pants fleeing Room 103. This woman actually picked another guy out of a lineup, he said, referring to Pak's identification of Michael Greco in Daegu.

He told Ofshe about Miss Yi, who had seen a man loitering outside the open door of Room 103 in the middle of the night. He told him about the exchange student in Room 102, Kati Peltomaa, who had heard an angry American male voice followed by the sounds of an assault.

What's more, he told Ofshe, is that the crime scene was very bloody, but there was no blood on Kenzi's clothes. On the morning Jamie's body was discovered, Kenzi was wearing the outfit everyone had seen her in the previous night. None of the other exchange students, nor the police officers, detectives or interpreters, noticed any blood on her clothes or her boots. Forensic analysis on the clothes a year later couldn't even find the smallest stain, he told Ofshe.

He also mentioned the blood smudge on the door leading out of the motel and the semen tests results, which were shaky because of the antiquated testing methods, but in the official record nonetheless.

Weis also told him that some of the contradictions that Mansfield found in Kenzi's statements seemed explainable. Maybe, for example, Vincent and Martinez were too drunk to remember seeing her. Maybe Jamie's panties were inside her jeans because she had another visitor after Kenzi departed. Perhaps Jamie had pulled on her clothes to answer a knock at the door, invited that person in and then undressed again—this time removing her panties and jeans together. The lack of water in the bathtub could be linked to the damp, bloody rag found near Jamie's body, Weis speculated. Perhaps the killer had used the rag to clean up hair or fingerprints or blood in the bathroom and soaked up the water too. After all, the agents questioned Kenzi about the rag, but she was never able to explain its presence, he noted.

The motive seemed suspect to Weis as well. The agents had come to Huntington with a prepackaged motive, and lo and behold, Kenzi confessed to that motive. As another defense attorney would later say, lesbian rage was "the sort of thing that sounds great in a frat house, but laughable to real women."

Ofshe was interested and said he would meet with Kenzi in person. Weis certainly must have been glad for the expert to take the case, but he also must have been worried about whether Kenzi fit the profile of a false confession. She had admitted the murder to authorities on three occasions in one month—twice in the Ramada and a third time in the lockup after waiving her Miranda rights. She had never accused the agents of beating her or even threatening her with violence, and now, in her jail cell, she wasn't exactly proclaiming her innocence. She freely admitted that the day she was arrested half of her was convinced she had killed Jamie, and when she spoke of her confession these days, it was in amorphous terms that were a far cry from an emphatic denial.

I have two competing memories, she would say. The one in which I am innocent had sounds and smells and sensations. The one in which I'm guilty is like a silent movie, images but no other sensations.

* * *

No one wants to believe that false confessions occur through psychological coercion. Torture is one thing, but if a totally innocent person can be coerced with mere words into admitting a gruesome crime, it seems to say something disturbing about human beings. It makes people weak and their memories malleable.

In the last decade, however, a series of well-publicized cases has left no doubt these confessions sometimes happen. In 1998, a fifteen-year-old teenager in San Diego, Michael Crowe, and a high school classmate confessed after lengthy interrogations to stabbing his sister to death as she slept in the family home. On the eve of trial, DNA tests showed spots of the victim's blood on the shirt of a mentally ill drifter caught wandering near the home the night of the murder. The charges against the boys were dropped, and the homeless man was later convicted in the girl's death.

Perhaps the best known case is that of the five teenagers convicted of attacking a jogger in Central Park in 1989. During protracted interrogations, all five youths confessed to beating up the woman, although they gave contradictory stories. In 2002 a violent sex offender came forward to say that he was the actual rapist. DNA tests bore out his statement.

Experts like Ofshe have documented scores of other cases. Much of the law enforcement community remains skeptical. Many rank and file detectives who interrogate suspects on a daily basis simply do not accept the idea of false confessions. Even in the two most prominent cases, Crowe and the jogger teens, some investigators still refuse to believe they got the wrong men—even in the face of DNA results. In the San Diego case, some involved in the investigation say privately they remain convinced Crowe and his friends are guilty and that the homeless man is just a scapegoat. In the jogger case, a report by the NYPD suggested the teens had initiated the attack and the rapist who came forward was the last in a string of assailants.

There are, of course, those in law enforcement who concede that false confessions sometimes happen. Some states, including Minnesota, Alaska and Illinois, and many local jurisdictions now require videotaping of interrogations in serious crimes to eliminate any question of whether a confession was coerced. Neither the FBI nor the army, however, videotape interviews. Even those in law enforcement who are concerned about coercion disagree strenuously with Ofshe and other experts about how often it occurs. They say they are extremely rare, but that when they do happen, the massive press coverage leads the public to believe they are more common than is actually the case.

While maintaining that they occur "regularly," Ofshe and others agree that there is no feasible way to determine their frequency. A researcher would need to know the number of interrogations that occur every year, the number of confessions that result and the number of those confessions that are eventually proved false.

"No one with a brain says they know," Ofshe says.

Researchers have identified two types of false confessions. The first and more frequent type is known as the compliant false confession. In these situations, a suspect knows he is innocent, but confesses because he believes his situation is hopeless, and telling the police what they want to hear will result in better treatment than maintaining innocence. Police have often lied to these suspects about the evidence, which is legal, and told them they have DNA or eyewitnesses that establish their guilt beyond a reasonable doubt. In some cases, the suspect believes he will be allowed to go home once he tells police what they want to hear. In others, the suspect thinks he will be wrongly but inevitably convicted, and a confession will make for a lighter sentence.

In the second type of confession, known as a persuaded false confession, the same fake evidence and sense of hopelessness exist, but their impact is different. The innocent person comes to believe that he actually committed the crime and confesses because he considers himself guilty. In these cases, the person comes to distrust his memories and concludes that he must have blacked out the offense. In some cases, these people believe they carried out the crimes during an alcohol- or drug-induced blackout.

Before he traveled east that summer, Ofshe asked Kenzi to write out an account of her confession. I want to know how she went from saying she didn't do it to saying she did, he told her lawyer. Ofshe requested as detailed a description as possible, and Kenzi sat for hours in her cell writing out a chronology of the confession in longhand.

DiVittis had written a brief summary of his interview, and Mansfield had filed a report of the confession's contents, but what Kenzi wrote out for Ofshe was the first extended account of the confession.

She wrote that when DiVittis and Mansfield accused her of murder on the second day of the interview, she had been shocked. She said she insisted that she had nothing to do with Jamie's death, but DiVittis told her that they knew she had done it. She said he told her they wanted to help her remember what she had done. She wrote that he suggested she might have blocked out what happened because it was just too gruesome.

"Sometimes as a defense mechanism when something is too much for the brain to handle, it will create a memory over a memory, try to patch things up and make the memory how we want it to be," she quoted DiVittis as telling her.

She said that he told her that if she couldn't recall what she had actually done, maybe they could get at the truth by talking about what she had felt. Remembering emotions, he said, might come more easily than remembering actions.

"He proceeded to ask me how I felt about females. Did I feel lust? Excitement? Anger? I couldn't really answer. I had never put a feeling to it," she wrote. "He then asked more 'specifically,' 'How did you feel when Jamie undressed for you that night?' ... [He] then asked me if I liked what I saw."

Kenzi said she hesitated and told DiVittis that she really didn't know what he was getting at. She said he appeared frustrated and the tone of the interview changed. If you won't go the emotional route, we'll have to do this the hard way, by actions, she quoted him as saying.

She said he asked how Jamie had taken off her clothes, and she repeated what she had told investigators before: She took off Jamie's shirt and pants and then left. She said he told her that was a lie. She said he asked again how Jamie had taken off her clothes, and she again said she did not know since she was not in

the room. She said DiVittis accused her again of lying,
this time in a sterner voice. Where was Jamie when
she took off her bra? she said he asked. This time, he
held up a photo of Jamie's bra on the bathroom floor,
she wrote. Where did she take off her bra? he asked.
Kenzi said she paused, looked at the photo and said, In
the bathroom. She said he replied, That's right, and
then quickly moved on to another question.

She said he asked if Jamie had taken off her pants
in a seductive manner. Kenzi said she once again told
him she didn't know because she was not in the room.
That's a lie, he told her. We know you were there. Try
to remember. Did she shimmy out of her pants? She
wrote that he showed her the photo of Jamie's panties
inside her pants. I guess she took them off at the same
time, she recalled telling him.

According to Kenzi, the same pattern was repeated
with dozens more leading questions. She first denied
the incriminating assertion in DiVittis's question, he
rejected the denial as a lie, and then he asked her the
question again with more forceful words and sometimes with a photo from the crime scene. In the statement she wrote for Ofshe, Kenzi said she eventually
accepted the idea that she might have repressed killing
Jamie, and that each time DiVittis asked her one of his
leading questions, she scoured her mind for an answer.

"I was slouched down in a chair with my eyes closed,
trying to find the memories," she wrote.

She said her mind was a big black empty space, and
as she thought harder, it would become gray, then white,
and images would appear. The images were like still
photos of her and Jamie in different positions in Room
103, she wrote. She said her mind flipped through the

images as if looking at a small photo album until she landed on one that fit the scenario suggested by DiVittis's questions: Jamie naked before her. Jamie in the bathtub. Jamie bloody and staring up at her.

"The whole session was mostly him asking questions, me pausing, trying to fight the black void in my head. Seeing pictures appearing [and] then disappearing," she wrote.

When she finally fixed on one image that seemed to go along with the question DiVittis was posing—whether it was Jamie shimmying out of her pants or her naked body on the floor—she described it to him as if it were a memory, he accepted it and they moved on to another question, she said.

She wrote that when she stumbled in trying to explain why she had killed Jamie, DiVittis told her that they needed to find the "trigger" that had caused her rage. There's something in your background that explains this, he told her. What could it be that would make you feel this scared and angry? She said she searched her mind for troubling events in her childhood and found an incident at day care when she was young and some boys had tried to look up her skirt. I didn't want to be naked in front of Jamie the same way I didn't want to be naked in front of the boys, she told DiVittis.

She said that by the end of the second day, she had come to believe that the images she found when questioned by DiVittis were reality and the memories she had held in the year since Jamie's murder—memories of being an innocent witness rather than a perpetrator—were false. This realization came to her in what she described as an almost trancelike state.

"I can't give precise details because it was like a dream," she wrote.

When she had written the final page, she mailed her statement to Ofshe at Berkeley. The professor had sought interviews with the agents as well, but the FBI and the army turned down his requests. Kenzi was his only source for details about the events inside the Ramada and she could hardly be called an unbiased narrator. Facing extradition and a possible death sentence, she had every reason to make the interview out to be as coerced as possible.

But perhaps surprisingly, the story Kenzi wrote out for Ofshe did not differ significantly from the accounts the three investigators would later give. In testimony and interviews, the men echoed her basic chronology of the confession. They recalled many of the same exchanges between DiVittis and Kenzi, sometimes word for word. They agreed that she was slouched down in a chair with her eyes shut for much of the interview, and they remembered DiVittis asking questions over and over until he got an answer.

All three men made clear that they thought her repression claims were bogus and that she was simply grabbing a face-saving lifeline DiVittis had thrown to her, but Lee acknowledged that she repeatedly muttered about murky memories before giving DiVittis answers.

"It's foggy, I can't see, I can't remember," he recalled her saying.

Four years later, in a conference room at FBI headquarters in Washington, D.C., Lee described watching the interrogation as a breathtaking, almost supernatural experience. The ebb and flow between Kenzi's denying and admitting was so dramatic that at one point, he and Mansfield snuck out of the room and into the motel hallway to regain their composure.

"What is happening here? This is so bizarre," he remembered them saying to each other.

Returning to the room, he felt electricity in the room.

"The hair on the back of my neck stood," he said.

Mansfield recounted a similar mix of excitement and dread.

"We had dedicated most of our waking hours to this investigation for the better part of seven months . . . we were beginning to understand what took place that night, and it was very important to us, not to mention the impact it was going to have on the Penich family," he recalled.

Kenzi Snider's written account of the confession was particularly fascinating to Richard Ofshe because of its focus on repressed memories. Before studying coerced confessions, Ofshe's specialty was cases where adults claimed to recover memories of childhood sexual abuse and other horrors. In the late 1980s and early 1990s, there were high-profile cases where children accused parents, day care workers and others of rape, murder and satanic worship during their youth. Ofshe concluded most if not all of these cases were bogus and that psychotherapists were planting the "memories" in their patients' heads through hypnosis, dream analysis and other means. In 1996 he coauthored *Making Monsters: False Memories, Psychotherapy and Sexual Hysteria,* which lambasted counselors who claimed to be helping clients recover memories of abuse. After reading Kenzi's statement, he wondered if Kenzi's interrogation had been a condensed version of this noxious therapy.

In August 2002 he flew to Charleston and drove to the jail. Guards led him to a small interview room where Kenzi was waiting. He looked at the tall, blond young woman with bright blue eyes and eager smile and felt an immediate sense of compassion.

"These people, I know what's happened to them better than they do," he recalls four years later. "I understood how she had been manipulated. I sympathized with her plight. I realized that she did not comprehend what had happened to her, but I also realized it wasn't my job to educate her."

Ofshe turned on his tape recorder and began questioning her. She told him about her dueling memories of the night of Jamie's murder and about how one felt like a real memory and the other like a silent movie.

"She was very conflicted about what was real," Ofshe remembers. He placed her in the second type of coerced confession, the persuaded false confession, where an innocent person comes to believe he committed the crime.

"One of the things that was unique about her, though, is that she never fully accepted the idea that she committed the crime, but she never fully dismissed it either," he says. "I guess it is sort of a tribute to her honesty."

After reviewing the chronology of the confession once more, he asked her about her background. Specifically, he wanted to know about anything that

might predispose her to DiVittis's suggestions or hypnosis in general.

She told him that she had read about repression in a
textbook for an introduction to psychology course. She
also mentioned that she had taken a couple of yoga
classes in which the instructor talked about "mind-
emptying" as a method of relaxation. Finally, she noted
an unusual nighttime ritual she had as a child: She
would listen to classical music as she fell asleep and
visualize animated scenes in her mind to accompany
the music.

"Like in the movie *Fantasia*," she told him.

Days after he interviewed Kenzi, Ofshe sent a report
to her lawyer calling her confession "deeply troubling
for a number of reasons." He said the fact that it rested
on the concept of a repressed memory made it "utterly
worthless" as evidence.

". . . Miss Snider's so-called confession is founded
on the existence of a mental mechanism [repression]
that has been discredited and rejected by the scientific
community," he wrote, pointing readers in a footnote
to a variety of sources on recovered memories, including his own book.

He took direct aim at the investigators' contention
that Kenzi was simply making up the repressed memory claim so she could confess with a small amount of
face-saving.

"How was it that a woman who had supposedly committed a murder, who was able to successfully lie to
Korean police and (probably) to American military investigators the day after the killing, who successfully
eluded arrest for 11 months and who had sufficient
control over her guilt to interact with her victim's for-

mer fiancé could be gotten to confess? Surely, someone who could carry off the deceptions attributed to Ms. Snider would have sufficient nerve to resist an accusation by three investigators who had not one shred of hard evidence to back up their accusation," he wrote.

He said that the confession investigators got reflected only their own preconceived notions. They came in thinking they could get her to say she had repressed the memory and lo and behold, she said she had repressed the memory. They came in thinking they could get her to say she and Jamie were experimenting sexually, and lo and behold, she says she and Jamie were experimenting sexually. They came in thinking they could get her to admit to murder, and voilà, she admitted to murder, he argued.

"[I]t is my opinion that the inculpatory statements she made on February 4th, 5th and 6th and March 1, 2002 are far more likely to be the product of the interrogation methods used by Agents DiVittis, Mansfield and Lee than they are to be statements based on Ms. Snider's personal knowledge of her participation in the murder of Jamie Penich," he wrote.

He said the agents had used the usual formula for false confessions: legal coercion and hopelessness. They told Kenzi they had proof she was the killer, and said they would not accept anything from her but incriminating statements.

"The tactics of the interrogation caused Ms. Snider to come to distrust the reliability of her memory and thereby to become confused about whether or not she had killed Ms. Penich," he wrote.

Ofshe wrote that Kenzi had slipped into a trance during DiVittis's questioning, perhaps because she was predisposed due to her experience with yoga and the nightly *Fantasia* visualizations, or what he grandly termed "Ms. Snider's almost decade long experience with self-hypnotic visualization and mind-emptying techniques."

He wrote that the best way to gauge a confession's truthfulness is to see whether the account the person confessing gave fit the evidence. Did he or she know information only the killer would know? That test "for fit" with the evidence was even more imperative in this case, he said, because Kenzi knew the victim well and had an intimate view of the crime scene before police arrived.

"Miss Snider's confession is difficult to evaluate for fit because of the failure to record it and because Ms. Snider reports that the interrogators grossly contaminated her knowledge of the crime by deliberately educating her as to the answers that they wanted on various points related to crime scene facts," he said.

CHAPTER 19

NOT BY THE MEMORIES
I HOLD TRUE

Ofshe's report was an unwelcome development for the federal prosecutors preparing for the extradition proceedings. The standard of evidence required for an extradition was minimal, but without forensic evidence or eyewitnesses against Kenzi, anything that shook the confession was worrisome. They put out a few calls to colleagues in other jurisdictions and learned about Ofshe and his reputation in law enforcement circles. Great, they said to one another, she got a hired gun and he delivered exactly the expert opinion she paid for.

Carefully reading his report, the prosecutors zeroed in on what he said was the hallmark of a true confession: independent corroborating evidence. Let's under-

mine this guy with his own advice, they said. Get a
laundry list of the corroborating evidence together,
they told Mansfield and Lee.

That fall, the army had transferred Mansfield back to
the United States. Lee remained in Korea. They quickly
responded to the request, however. Mansfield said he
considered all the contradictions that had led him to
focus on Kenzi corroborating evidence in that the confession explained them. Her statement confirmed the
bartender's memory of the American girls leaving
Nickleby's closer to 1:30 A.M. than 3:15 A.M. It confirmed
Vincent's claim that he never saw them on the street. It
confirmed the lack of water in the tub. It was consistent
with Jeroen's statement that she only climbed over him
into bed once. It was consistent with the way Jamie's
clothes were arranged in the bathroom.

All those points were problematic for the prosecution, however, because the investigators had used them
to confront Kenzi, and once they shared them with her
in the course of the interrogation, they lost their value
as independent and spontaneous corroboration. Ofshe
could claim Kenzi was simply incorporating information they provided into her confession.

Undeterred, Lee and Mansfield turned to three points
in her confession that were not open to that criticism.
First was a linear bruise stretching across Jamie's back
from one underarm to the other. The mark had puzzled
investigators since the autopsy. There was nothing under her body on the bedroom floor that would have
caused such a mark. Kenzi's confession offered an explanation. She said she had tripped as she dragged Jamie by the underarms out of the bathroom. Jamie had
landed hard on her back on the small step separating

the bathroom from the foyer. The bruise had never been publicized, and Kenzi had no reason to say she had dropped Jamie unless it was the truth.

Secondly, there was the jacket on Jamie's face. In her confession, Kenzi said that as she was stomping down on Jamie, her foot touched something soft on the floor and she picked it up and used it to cover Jamie's head. Although Kenzi had seen the jacket on Jamie's face when she ran into Room 103 the morning of the murder, the statement explained something that was not widely known: There was a partial boot print in blood on the jacket.

Third, there were three small parallel bruises, like stripes, along Jamie's right cheek line. To the investigators, the bruises seemed to confirm Kenzi's account of the backhanded slap that rendered Jamie unconscious. After they had provided this list to the prosecutors, Lee—apparently trying to shore up this final point—contacted Dr. Yang, the coroner who had performed the autopsy at NISI. Could the three bruises have been caused by a backhand slap? he asked.

A few days later, Dr. Yang gave him a disappointing answer. In a faxed letter, he wrote that the bruises were caused by something other than a blow from a human hand. The bruises were three to four millimeters apart. The bones in the human hand are normally ten millimeters apart, he wrote.

He told Lee that he had studied the crime scene photographs for something that could have caused the distinctive mark. A short ledge of ribbed rubber dividing the foyer from the bedroom seemed a good candidate, he wrote.

"There's a possibility that the three parallel lines of

bruise in the area of the right lower jaw may have been
made by this rubber material because it has similar
width and the distance of convex and concave area," he
wrote.

It appeared that someone had ground Jamie's jaw
against that ledge, he said. Four years later, Lee says he
can't recall if he ever received the fax from Dr. Yang.
In any case, he never told prosecutors about the coroner's conclusions.

On October 2, 2002, all the parties in the case de-
scended on Huntington for a two-day extradition hearing. As for the bail hearing, television trucks parked
outside the federal courthouse and reporters came from
Charleston and Pittsburgh. The assistant U.S. attorneys,
Larry Ellis and Philip Wright, drove down from Charleston, as did Weis, Kenzi's public defender. DiVittis arrived from Cleveland and Mansfield from his new
posting in Atlanta. Both were staying in the Ramada.
Kenzi's brothers came in from Rhode Island and Minnesota. Her mother flew in from Thailand. They sat with
her college friends, who had cut class and walked or
carpooled downtown from campus. The Penichs made
the five-hour drive through the mountains from Derry
and sat across from the Sniders and their many support-
ers in the hall. Patty watched Kenzi's mother in particular. Heath Bozonie chatted amiably with her sons and
Kenzi's friends. As the Sniders invariably did, Heath
seemed friendly, upbeat, and determined to remain calm
and take everything in stride.

"I walked past her [mother] in the hall," Patty Penich
remembered. "I thought about saying something. It's

not her fault. But then I thought, what am I going to say? 'Hi, your daughter killed my daughter.' I didn't say anything."

One person who was not in the courtroom was Kenzi's father. Years later, he says he did not know the hearing was taking place.

"We really are not in the best contact," he says matter-of-factly.

Since her arrest that spring, there had been whispers about her father. In nearly every conversation about the case, a point would come when one person would lower his voice and ask, "You know about her dad, right?"

Three months before Kenzi went to Korea, her father told her he was gay. Her parents had been divorced for a couple of years, and she was making a rare visit to Florida to spend Thanksgiving with him and her older brother. He invited her to lunch.

"It was strange because my father and I had never had lunch alone before. I still remember I was eating tomato soup and he said, 'You know my friend Pete? Well, he's more than a friend,'" she recalled.

Roger Snider said that he realized during the course of his marriage that he was gay, but that he never acted on it. He maintains somewhat incredibly that his homosexuality had nothing to do with the breakup of his marriage.

"We grew apart, and the last ten years there was no communication. It wasn't because I was gay, it was because it always went back to the same recriminations and what should have been," he said. His wife did not want him to leave the air force and never let him forget it, he said.

The year the divorce was final, he came out to a

friend. He was living in Florida, away from his four children and ex-wife, and did not inform them. For years, he was openly gay with friends and neighbors, but never announced it to his family. He didn't exactly camouflage it, however. He brought his partner, Pete, to his son Jordan's wedding and introduced him as a friend who had helped him with the long drive to Minnesota. When Jordan and his wife, Katie, visited him at his house in Florida, she remembered, "he had that purple Teletubby in his bathroom, and he kept talking about his drapes and whether the color was right. And there was an *Out* Magazine . . . on his table."

Kenzi says that when her father got around to telling her during the Thanksgiving 2000 trip, she was surprised, but not troubled.

"It was never the Waltons," she says. "We weren't close, and I didn't know lots of things about him. I didn't know what his favorite color was and I didn't know this."

She says she saw some of her father's decisions in a new light. He had married the girl next door, joined the air force and stayed as far away from home as possible. Maybe he was running from his true self, she thought.

In the weeks afterward, she told her father repeatedly that he should inform her mother and her two brothers, who did not yet know. She was exceptionally close to her mother and knew she would be troubled by the news. Finally, she gave her father a deadline of January 19. It's a date she still remembers.

Tell them by then or I will, she says she told him.

The deadline came and went, and Kenzi told her mother and brother Roman over dinner at Pizza Hut. The news stung Heath Bozonie initially, but in true

Snider fashion, she says that she quickly looked at it as a welcome development.

"I always wondered what I was doing wrong, why things didn't work, and this explained everything," she says.

Her brother Durham found out soon after and says "it wasn't a big deal at all."

Like his mother, he says the disclosure had a positive side.

"It shed light on a few things. He was like constantly in a bad mood, which makes sense if he isn't happy and he isn't getting any sort of satisfaction and is in absolutely the wrong relationship than he is supposed to be in," he says.

Kenzi says she was relieved that her mother and brothers knew even though she had angered her father by telling them. She says that whatever family tension existed stemmed not from her father being gay, but from him not being open about it.

Still, she talked a lot about it with her friends, and it was one of the things she revealed in late-night bull sessions with the other exchange students in Korea.

During the first phase of the interrogation, before the investigators accused her, DiVittis asked her a series of questions designed to suggest the lesbian theme. Among the questions was how she felt about homosexuals. She told the investigators then about her father and said that she had no biases against gays.

Mansfield's notes of her initial confession include a reference to her father. It is just one line, but it is very powerful. In the middle of describing kissing and stroking Jamie, Mansfield quoted Kenzi as saying, "That would make me like my dad. I don't like my dad."

To some, including Jamie's relatives and some of the exchange students, her father's homosexuality seemed very germane to the case. Perhaps the revelation had made her somehow both attracted and repulsed by gay sex. Maybe she started something with Jamie and then hated herself for it. When Roger Snider first heard about the confession, even he briefly wondered whether his own gayness had played some sort of role.

"I considered it, but not for long. She grew up in my house, I know what she's capable of," he said.

Her friends and family were dismissive.

Jen Thompson, a friend from St. Cloud, said she thought of the many gay friends they had in common.

"It just didn't make sense," she says.

Her brother Jordan rolls his eyes whenever anyone suggests it was a motive for murder.

"All four kids found out. Why didn't the others kill anyone?" he says.

At 9:30 A.M. on October 2, 2002, Magistrate Maurice Taylor mounted an unfamiliar bench in an unfamiliar courtroom in the Sidney L. Christie Federal Building in Huntington and took in an unfamiliar scene. Before him was a courtroom three times as large and fifty times as elaborate as the plain, functional courtroom where he worked on his docket of search warrant applications, bail hearings and misdemeanor trials. The room, which was generally reserved for district court judges and their federal felony or civil trials, had a ceiling higher than many churches, elaborate white molding, brocaded ivory wallpaper and twenty-foot windows with red velvet drapes. The spectators who packed the six long rows of the gallery stared back at him.

It was a rare occasion for Taylor to do anything unfamiliar in the Christie Building. The sixty-year-old, a native West Virginian, had served as a magistrate there for twenty-six years. Before that, he was a defense attorney in its courtrooms, representing moonshiners and car thieves, and not long before that, he had been a clerk for Judge Sidney Christie.

Now he was about to preside over his first extradition hearing. When assistant U.S. attorney Larry Ellis observed that the proceeding was "a little bit of a different kettle of fish for us here in the Southern District of West Virginia," Taylor had to agree.

He knew that in some jurisdictions this sort of hearing would take a magistrate a few minutes, but everything was new to him and the lawyers, and he wanted to get it right. For weeks he had been reading old extradition cases, some stretching back to the early years of the United States. Among the issues he had to resolve was what parts of the case file the defense was entitled to. In a murder trial, the prosecutor would be required to provide Kenzi's lawyers with any exculpatory material, but in an extradition hearing, there was no such obligation. Her lawyer, however, said the specifics of the case demanded he know about evidence investigators had pointing away from her, and after some squabbling with prosecutors, Taylor ordered them to hand over anything that was favorable to her case. That should have included the letter the Korean pathologist wrote to Lee a month before, debunking the three-bruise theory, but for whatever reason, the prosecutors never received it and in turn never gave it to the defense.

With the defense calling the confession into question at the hearing, Taylor's focus was on determining whether Kenzi's statements were solid enough to meet the probable cause burden—enough evidence to establish that there was a fair probability she killed Jamie.

In his opening statement, Ellis told the magistrate he should ignore the defense allegations about Kenzi's confession.

"Nothing in her confession is factually impossible. Nothing in her confession is absurd. This is not a confession of having killed Trotsky or committing murder by voodoo," he said. "Snider is a well-educated, competent functioning person."

He said the issue of repression was a red herring offered up by Ofshe.

"It's not our position that she repressed memories. It's just . . . how she told the story," he said.

In his remarks to the judge, Kenzi's public defender, Weis, said the evidence pointed to another killer. He referred to the semen police detected on Jamie's body and the fact no one saw blood on Kenzi's pants legs after the murder.

"This is not a sophisticated criminal. This is a person with no record, with good character, who hasn't been in trouble before, who is supposed to have pulled the wool over everyone's eyes for eleven months in all her contact with police, in all her contact with Jamie's fiancé. That just does not make sense," he told Taylor.

Prosecutors called the FBI agent who took Kenzi's statement after her arrest and then Mansfield. Dressed in his uniform, Mansfield took the stand and explained how he built the case against Kenzi in Korea. He described the contradictions, the water and sound tests in the Kum Sung and his decision to confront Kenzi. He described the confession as he saw it from his vantage point on the floor behind her and gave most of the credit to the more experienced DiVittis.

"It's a stressful thing when you've been on a case that long, and it felt good for him to be in charge of it," he said.

Under questioning by Ellis, he ticked off the ways in which he said her confession corroborated the evidence: the linear bruise on Jamie's back, the bloody boot print on the jacket and the three bruises on Jamie's chin. Lee was not at the hearing and the prosecutors did not know that Dr. Yang had dismissed the theory that the bruises were caused by a backhand blow.

On cross-examination, Weis asked Mansfield if he was equipped to recognize a false confession if he saw one.

"[A]re you given any training on what to do or what you should not do so as to avoid a false confession?" the lawyer asked.

"Not that I am aware of. Nothing I can recall," Mansfield replied.

Weis suggested the motive for the murder was illogical.

"Anyone ever tell you that Kenzi or Jamie were aggressive lesbians?" Weis asked.

"Absolutely not," Mansfield answered.

"Anyone ever tell you that Kenzi and Jamie had a lesbian affair prior to the murder," he asked.

"No," Mansfield replied.

When the investigator implied Kenzi had been in a trance when she confessed "as if she's describing a movie which she is seeing or performing," Mansfield shook his head.

"I couldn't agree with you on a movie. It's in and out. Sometimes it's that way, and then it rolls with a lot of information that's spontaneous and meets with the characteristics of the crime scene. So I'd have a hard time to agree with you that it's like a movie she's watching," he testified.

Weis grilled him about the evidence pointing to another killer, including the lack of bloody clothes, Pak's sighting of a man fleeing the motel, Yi's memory of a man loitering outside Room 103 and Kati's account of hearing an angry American male's voice and the sounds of an assault. Mansfield admitted that he could not explain why there was no blood visible on Kenzi's pants and why Kati had heard males at about the time of the murder. He suggested, however, that Yi and Pak gave stories that did not match and were fundamentally unreliable.

With his account, the government rested, and Weis called an unexpected defense witness: DiVittis. The FBI agent was as experienced in the witness box as he was in the interrogation room. He knew how to answer a defense lawyer's questions. He was precise and refused to fall into traps like agreeing to overbroad principles or giving opinions instead of facts. He acknowledged the "minimizing" and face-saving techniques he had employed, but he jousted with the defense lawyer whenever he implied DiVittis's questioning might lead to a confession that was false or coerced.

"You're undermining their confidence in their true memory. That is, in fact, what you are doing," Weis charged.

"No, because if someone is having a true memory, you will see in body language, you will see in statements, and you will see in demeanor that this person is not being deceptive," he said.

"[Y]ou are saying that I am trying to undermine their confidence in truth. No. I want the truth. So I don't undermine truth. I undermine deceit, saying it's not worth lying anymore, because the truth is what we want," he said.

Weis asked him whether he agreed with the bureau's policy of not taping interviews, and DiVittis said he did.

"I don't think people would understand an interrogation. My opinion is that they wouldn't understand what is going on. So, you know, why put the family through that? Why let people look at something and get confused over something when what comes out of it is 'I killed her. This is how I killed her,' and they've signed a statement," he said.

He added, "It is not important for me whether she's saying, 'I killed her because I don't like blue birds' or 'I did it for this reason' or 'I did it for that.' That is not important. What's important is she killed her."

During a brief cross-examination, prosecutor Ellis asked, "Did you put anything in her mouth about details about how Jamie Penich was killed?"

"No," he replied.

"Did you ask her at one point why was it so clear for her now?" Ellis continued.

"Yes," he said.

"What was her response?"

" 'Because it's the truth,' " he answered.

The defense also called Ofshe as a witness. He

reiterated the findings in his report, telling the magistrate that what Kenzi had confessed to were "pseudo-memories" created during the interrogation and not independent memories.

Ellis was well prepared to attack Ofshe's credibility. He noted that the expert had been involved in a messy lawsuit against the American Psychological Association in 1992. He pointed out errors in his report about the Penich case, including a reference to the blood on the door handle leading out of the Kum Sung. Ofshe was under the impression the blood was Jamie's when tests showed it belonged to a man.

The prosecutor accused Ofshe of being a zealot who was more concerned about fixing the problem of false confessions than the facts of individual cases.

"You believe that false confessions are a pervasive problem in the American criminal justice system, don't you?" Ellis charged.

"Pervasive, no. I think they're a regularly occurring phenomenon," Ofshe replied.

"You've been very vocal about it, though haven't you?" the prosecutor continued.

"I think an innocent person sent to prison based on a false confession is a tragedy, whether it's one, ten, a thousand a year," Ofshe said.

The prosecutor also noted that the professor was being compensated for his testimony by the public defender's office.

"You are getting paid $8,000 for your service in this case," he reminded Ofshe.

At times, the questioning smacked of the culture wars between rural law and order and wealthy, liberal academia. Ellis repeatedly noted that Ofshe taught at Berkeley and also suggested he was getting rich off cases like the Jamie Penich murder.

In response to a query about his annual income from casework, Ofshe said, "I don't know the exact amount that I get paid for consultation. I think it's about maybe 40 percent of my total income, maybe less."

"Well, what would 40 percent of your total income be?" Ellis asked.

"I don't know," Ofshe said.

"You don't know how much money you make?"

"No."

"It's a nice way to be. You've got a new house you're building down in the Florida Keys?"

"No."

"No? But you don't know how much money you make?"

"No."

The dustup continued for hours, but Ofshe never budged from his conclusion that the confession was coerced.

The hearing's most-anticipated witness was Kenzi herself. She walked to the stand in her orange jumpsuit. In the witness box, she could look out at the spectators' gallery, something she was prohibited from doing at the defense table. She saw her family and friends, all together in one room to support her. She would say later that in those days, she felt a sense of great fortune because of her loved ones.

"It was like when Huck Finn and Tom Sawyer got to

see their own funeral," she recalled. "I got to see what I meant to other people and know what they meant to me."

During about two hours on the stand, she detailed the confession as she had to Ofshe. She spoke in a confident, strong voice. She said she still had "two stories" of the night of March 17.

"One feels like a memory," she testified.

"And what does the other one feel like?" Weis asked.

"A story," she replied.

She said she was "very confident" in the "memory" of leaving Jamie alive, but that the "story" of killing her "doesn't feel right. I'm not confident," she said.

Because DiVittis had told her she might have repressed memories, she struggled to uncover "forgotten" ones, she testified.

"They kept telling me I was wrong. So I was trying to find the right [memories]," Kenzi said. At the very end of her testimony, Weis posed the question that was intended to be the dramatic high point of her testimony.

"Did you kill Jamie?" he said.

The lawyer and everyone else in the hushed courtroom expected to hear a loud, unequivocal "No."

Instead, Kenzi replied, "Not by the memories I hold true."

In the courtroom, there was a ripple of surprise. Was it just a flowery turn of phrase from an unusual young woman? Or was she saying now after all this, that she still wasn't sure? People were uncertain.

At the prosecution table, the assistant U.S. attorneys

looked at each other, stunned. There is something so off about this girl, they thought.

In their final arguments, the prosecutors focused on what Kenzi didn't say. She didn't claim the agents beat her or threatened her or fed her information. Kenzi came up with the "shocking detail" of the confession on her own, Ellis argued. Kenzi Snider was not a child or mentally retarded when she gave the confession, the prosecutor said. He pointed out that she spoke several languages, had lived around the world, read Shakespeare and had aced her advanced placement classes. She was too smart and sophisticated to be coerced into falsely admitting to murder, he added. In closing, the prosecutor read the parts of confession that he said only the killer could know. He cited the bruise on Jamie's back, the bloody footprint on the jacket and once again, the three linear bruises that, he said, matched a backhand slap. With neither Lee nor the coroner in the courtroom, his assertion went unrefuted.

After the hearing, Taylor returned to his chambers. His first floor office is a huge rectangular room with an enormous desk and walls hung with works by artists from West Virginia, including a painting of a coal tippler in the mountain town where he was raised. After a week of mulling the evidence, Taylor issued his decision. Kenzi was to be extradited.

Echoing Ellis's argument, he wrote, "[Kenzi] is a well educated individual, and there is no evidence in the record before this Court that she suffers from psychological or other problems which might have caused her to confess falsely."

He cautioned that his decision was not a comment on

whether there was enough evidence for a conviction, just a determination that there was probable cause.

"The court concludes that The Republic of Korea has satisfied its burden of establishing probable cause to believe that Kenzi Noris Elizabeth Snider murdered Jamie Lynn Penich. The court, accordingly, finds that Ms. Snider is extraditable," he wrote.

CHAPTER 20

WHITE GOOD

That same month, on the other side of the world, investigators for the Seoul District Prosecutors' Office picked up a man for questioning in connection with two unsolved mob murders that were creeping toward the cold case files. The man, suspected of being a hit man for a crime syndicate in the city, had nothing to do with Jamie Penich's murder, but unbeknownst to Kenzi, still sitting in a jail cell awaiting extradition, his fate would be inextricably tied to hers. While she wrote pen pals and tutored other inmates, investigators working for the Seoul prosecutors conducted an all-night interrogation of the thirty-two-year-old man. When he would not confess, they beat him, apparently with a club. He slipped into unconsciousness and died.

Shortly after Magistrate Taylor ordered Kenzi Snider extradited, Weis received a call from a young man who said he had just learned of her situation from an article on the Internet. My name is Michael Greco and I believe I have important information about the case, he said to the defense lawyer.

"I told him I knew about some really sketchy stuff with the FBI and the army in Korea, and that I'd be willing to tell them about it," Greco recalled. "But I guess the extradition had already happened because he said, 'It's out of my hands. It's up to the Koreans now.' "

Greco, the University of Rhode Island exchange student briefly considered a suspect in Jamie's murder, hung up the phone and decided not to pursue the matter. It had been hard enough to make the call. A year had passed since his contact with Mansfield, Lee and the Koreans, but he had discussed the experience only with his immediate family and a few close friends. It was almost too upsetting to talk about.

Mansfield reached out to Greco two months after the army investigator took over the case, in the period just before he began focusing on Kenzi as the prime suspect. Greco, one of a handful of Americans studying at Keimyung, had known both Kenzi and Jamie. He and Kenzi, both nineteen, were the youngsters of the exchange group, and he and Jamie shared a passion for anthropology.

"People were getting along great. It's amazing how quickly you bond with people when you are foreigners in a strange environment. After two weeks, it felt like we had known each other for years," he recalled.

The group who planned the weekend jaunt to Seoul had invited him along, but he told them he had plans to meet his roommate's family for dinner that Saturday. After the murder, other students left the program, but Greco remained at Keimyung, the only American to do so. He and one of the students from the trip to Seoul, Russian Elvira Makhmoutova, began dating that spring.

On October 5, 2001, Mansfield and Lee made the three-hour trip to Daegu with a small contingent of Korean detectives. Greco, then in his second semester at Keimyung, was summoned to the international studies building by a school official and told the police had some questions about Jamie's death. Ushered into a conference room, Greco saw the two American agents, several Korean National Police officers, and a Korean woman who immediately caught his attention. She was an ajima, an older lady, and she was staring at him intently.

"I thought it was kind of weird because old ladies don't really do these types of jobs in Korea, but I thought maybe she knows some forensic stuff or something," he remembered. The woman was Chong-Sun Pak, the wife of the manager of the Kum Sung Motel. No one informed Greco that, as he sat at the conference table between the two American agents, he was effectively participating in a suspect lineup. Pak was on the trip to Daegu to look Greco up and down and tell police whether he was the man with the bloody pants she had seen fleeing the motel.

In his report of the meeting, Mansfield described Greco as behaving suspiciously from the start.

"AGENT'S COMMENT: Greco was extremely nervous at the beginning of the interview. He had accepted a cigarette from S[pecial] A[gent] Lee and began to smoke it, but it did not appear that Greco was a smoker," Mansfield typed later.

In an interview years later, however, Greco remembered feeling fine. He said it was Mansfield and Lee who kept telling him he seemed antsy and they who recommended he use the restroom. He said he did handle the cigarette awkwardly because he did not smoke, but thought it was rude to refuse a cigarette offered by an elder.

In any case, while Greco was in the men's room, Pak told them she was "99 percent sure" that he was the man with the bloody pants, according to Mansfield's report.

When Greco returned to the conference room, he immediately detected a more intense glare from the ajima.

"She was looking at me like I was a murderer," he said.

The agents' questions changed as well. Earlier, they had quizzed him about Jamie's enemies and her love interests, neither of which he knew her to have, he recalls, but when he returned, "It just turned into 'Where were you? Where were you? Where were you?'"

He explained that he was in Daegu the entire weekend of the murder. After a beef dinner with his roommate's parents, he met up with some friends for drinks and then went to bed, he said. Mansfield and Lee told him they had found his nametag in Jamie's purse and asked why it was there if he wasn't with her in Seoul.

Greco said he had no memory of giving Jamie the tag but said the exchange students wore nametags whenever they took field trips. In the two weeks before Jamie's death, he said, they went on several trips. It was possible he had wanted to take his nametag off on one of those occasions and had asked her to hold it for him.

As it grew into evening, the university buildings began to close, including the international students' office. The agents asked if he would consent to a search of his dorm room, and he agreed. Pak and one of the Korean officers went through his belongings, apparently looking for clothes that matched the ones worn by the man with the bloody pants.

Finding nothing, the American agents asked Greco to come with them to their hotel for more questioning.

"I was starting to wonder what was going on, but I thought, 'Hey, they're Americans. They must be on my side,'" Greco said.

At first, his instinct appeared correct. On the car ride to the hotel, he and the agents built a rapport, joking and talking about girls. But when they got into the room where the agents were staying, things changed swiftly, Greco recalled.

Mansfield directed him to a low chair by a coffee table. Lee and the Korean National Police detectives sat on the bed. Mansfield maneuvered a chair directly in front of Greco and sat down.

"The next thing I know Mark [Mansfield] leans across the table, looks me in the face, and says, 'We're not going to believe a thing you say until you tell us why you were in Seoul that night,'" Greco said.

He said the agent never raised his voice, but the aggression in his words terrified him.

"I don't think he actually lunged at me, but it felt like a lunge. My whole body went pins and needles. I almost blacked out," he said.

When he composed himself, he told them again that he was in Daegu, two hundred miles from Seoul, on the night of the murder.

"I said, 'You know I have a solid alibi,'" he remembered.

According to Greco, the investigators refused to believe him. They told him that the motel owner's wife had positively identified him.

"They started basically telling me a series of scenarios: 'Here's how you did it. Here's your motivation.' They came up with a couple of them. One was something about me going to visit Elvira [Makhmoutova] and knocking on the wrong door. It didn't even make sense," he said.

Mansfield pressed on, ignoring Greco's protests.

"They filled in the whole thing like it was a movie. It was detailed descriptions as to how I would've gone about it, time schedules for the train, how I would've found the motel, how I would've hit her, what the room looked like, everything," he added.

When he continued to maintain his innocence, he says, they offered him other choices: Perhaps it was an accident, or maybe he had repressed the memory of killing her.

"Maybe you're completely crazy and you don't remember it," he recalled them saying.

At that point, he says, his mind began to reel. The conversation became a circle with no escape. They accused, he denied, and they accused again. Had an hour passed, or was it five? Between him and the door were at least five officers. Because he was outside the United States and not technically in custody, he received no Miranda warning.

Still, he says, "I wanted a lawyer. From that time forward though, any time I brought up the topic, I was pretty much told, 'You don't need one. Don't worry about it.' They made me feel as though by getting a lawyer it would make things worse. It would make me look more guilty or something." Over time, Greco said, "I started thinking I have a better chance of saying I was in Seoul. Maybe they'll cut me some slack if I agree to this one thing."

He says he contemplated this partial confession for a few minutes, but ultimately decided he couldn't do it. There was just no way I was there, he told them. The interview ended as abruptly as it began.

Greco claims the investigators told him, "This isn't our standard policy, but why don't you come out and get some soju with us?" Soju is a strong Korean liquor similar to vodka. Greco was wary, but says they insisted. At a nearby bar and restaurant, they crowded around him at a table.

"We were drinking Korean style, which is shot after shot, and they were filling up my glass. In Korea, when someone fills up your glass, you have to drink it immediately. That's the honorable thing to do," he said.

Greco says he was still shaken by the interview and felt the alcohol going to his head. He excused himself and called his father, Ralph, in Rhode Island. It was the middle of the day at his father's manufacturing business in Providence, and the sound of his son's panicked voice jarred Ralph Greco. When he heard about the investigators and the questions, he became stern with the teenager.

"I said, 'Mike, these guys are not your friends. What are you doing with them?'" Ralph Greco recalled. "My concern was that they were not trying to solve the case so much as close it."

Ralph Greco insisted on speaking with the agents. His son returned to the table and handed the cell phone to Lee.

"My comment to him was, 'Shouldn't this kid have a lawyer? And what are you doing with him in a bar?' Mike wasn't even legal [to drink] here. And [Lee] said, 'No, no, he's just cooperating,'" Ralph Greco said.

"I insisted on leaving after that," Michael Greco recalled.

Early the next morning, Mansfield called Greco's apartment and asked him to give samples of his blood and hair and a cheek swab for DNA. He agreed.

"I knew that it would clear me," he says.

About three weeks later, the agents called again to say they had flown in a polygraph specialist from Hawaii. They wanted Greco to take a lie detector test.

"I said I don't think those things are very accurate. They told me if you really want to clear your name, that's what you have to do," he says. Greco agreed to the test, and Mansfield picked him up and drove him to a nearby U.S. army base.

"I bombed it, and they gave it to me again, and I bombed that one too," he recalled. The polygrapher wrote in his report that "the examinee was being deceptive when answering the relevant questions."

Later, after Kenzi became the lead suspect, authorities said Greco failed because he knew too much about the case from other students. But Greco believes he failed because of pressure from Mansfield and other investigators. He says that when they reviewed the test questions beforehand they insisted he change his answers to two minor questions: Have you ever wanted to hurt someone, and have you ever caused physical harm? Greco, who played football in high school and was in a fistfight in junior high, answered yes to both.

"They told me I had to say no," he recalls.

In effect, he says, they made him lie and then faulted him for failing the exam. Afterward, he phoned his father.

"I told him I had just failed a lie detector test and they thought I was the murderer," Greco said.

His father was furious.

"He told me I was a moron for taking the test," Greco recalls.

Mansfield drove Greco back to his dorm in silence. That night, Greco huddled in his apartment with a few friends. While they reassured him he wasn't going crazy, he lay on the floor in the fetal position crying. He was certain he would be arrested.

Surprisingly, he did not hear from Mansfield the next day, or the day after that. Weeks stretched into months. A few days before Christmas, he got a call from Mansfield. It was the end of the semester and Greco was packing his belongings to return to the United States.

According to Greco, Mansfield told him they had verified his alibi by giving a lie detector test to his roommate.

"It's all worked out," Greco remembers the agent saying.

The conversation occurred within days of Mansfield telling other investigators that Kenzi was probably the killer.

In early January, when he was back in Rhode Island, Greco got a call from Lee.

"He started asking about Kenzi. The spotlight was off me, but he wanted to know if she could possibly be a lesbian. Was she the type to come on to another girl," he recalled. He said he did not know Kenzi that well and got off the phone as quickly as possible.

Years later, Greco, a twenty-four-year-old residential counselor for troubled teens in Rhode Island, said he still struggles with his memories of the interrogation and recalls the terror he felt in the hotel room. But he has qualms about saying anything negative about the army or the FBI.

"I never want to go through that again," he said.

"I'm not the type of person who will say Kenzi did it or Kenzi didn't do it, because I don't know," Greco said.

"But I do know that the way they dealt with me is not the way I expected. And I can see it would lead someone in Kenzi's position to make a false confession," he said.

Mansfield's report about the interview does not include the interrogation in the hotel room or the trip to the bar. But informed of his allegations years later, neither Lee, nor Mansfield disputed much of what he said happened. They maintained, however, that he misinterpreted their motives.

"His perception that we were attempting to convince him he murdered Ms. Penich is a false one," Mansfield wrote in response to an e-mail asking about the incident.

He said it was the Korean National Police investigators' idea to take Greco to dinner after the interrogation and that in their culture, dinner necessarily meant drinks. He said he felt it was unprofessional and told them so, but when they insisted, he had no choice but to go along with it.

"It was their decision, and I felt at the time I would have disrespected them had I chosen to stand on the sidewalk in front of the restaurant and refuse to sit down at the table," he wrote.

Lee acknowledges that the agents "came down on [Greco] pretty hard," and perhaps should not have taken him to the bar. But, he says, unpleasant things happen during a murder investigation.

"Is this traumatic for Mike [Greco]? Yes, of course, but we have a 21-year-old girl who is dead here," he says.

He brushes off any suggestion that Greco's experience might indicate that Kenzi's confession was coerced. The proof, he says, was that, despite an intense grilling, Greco insisted on his innocence.

"Would you confess to murder if you didn't do it? The bottom line is, he didn't," Lee says.

By New Year's Eve 2002, Kenzi Snider was in solitary confinement in Youngdeungpo Detention Center in Seoul. While revelers outside celebrated the turn of the calendar, she sat on the floor of her four-by-seven-foot cell. Voices echoed through a distant cellblock, but she could not understand them. The two weeks of beginner Korean she had taken almost two years before proved of little assistance. On the cell wall hung a sheet of paper listing items for sale in the commissary, but she could not decipher the characters.

The cell had one window that looked out on a wall and a tree. The window had no bars, but it did have an ornamental gate that partially obscured the view. It reminded her of the diplomatic compounds where she had grown up.

"It was pretty in a way," she remembers.

She had arrived in Korea on December 20, two months after the Huntington magistrate approved her extradition. Kenzi chose not to file a habeas corpus petition challenging the ruling because she believed an appeal would just delay the inevitable. Accompanied by two U.S. marshals, she took a nonstop commercial flight from Washington, D.C., to Seoul. Because the trip was fifteen hours, the marshals were entitled to fly first class and Kenzi sat between them in the last row of the plush cabin watching businessmen pick at shrimp cocktails and puff pastry. The marshals had removed her shackles and handcuffs, and neither the passengers nor the flight attendants knew that the pretty, blond twenty-one-year-old was a suspected killer, let alone the first American ever extradited to South Korea.

After the flight touched down at Incheon International Airport, Kenzi and the marshals remained seated as the other passengers filed out of the aircraft. When the last one was gone, a familiar face ducked his head into the plane. It was Lee. With Mansfield now transferred to a CID office in Kansas, the FBI agent was the lead American on the case. As he boarded the plane that day, he was serving two functions, shepherding his case toward a successful prosecution and acting as Kenzi's bilingual guide through the Korean justice system.

Lee had not been in West Virginia for the extradition hearing, but he had of course heard that she had recanted the confession. It had been difficult for him to believe. Despite the confession, Lee respected Kenzi as an honest, good-hearted person. He felt he saw her true self in the remorse and tears in the Ramada. Looking down at her in the airplane seat, he believed there was still hope she would do the right thing.

It was Lee's task to walk Kenzi through Korea's legal system, a complex machine quite different from America's. The differences hit her just two days after her flight touched down. Before she appeared before a judge or met with her lawyer, Lee and the police came to her cell, placed her in handcuffs and then tied heavy blue ropes around her wrists and waist. They helped her into a police vehicle and drove her to Itaewon to the door of the Kum Sung Motel. The Korean detectives spoke to her firmly, and Lee translated.

"You are going to reenact your crime," he explained.

She was taken aback.

"I don't understand," she told him.

He said that she would have to pantomime exactly what she had confessed to doing the night of the murder. But the confession I gave is wrong, she told him. Lee sighed. If you want, he told her, you can act out both an "innocent" and a "guilty" version of events.

Surrounded by uniformed officers, she retraced her movements on March 17, 2001. Officers snapped photos as she led them up the street past the Dunkin' Donuts and the Burger King to the Indian restaurant where she and the other exchange students had dined. The streets of Itaewon were crowded with Christmas shoppers who stared at the young white woman bound in heavy ropes and surrounded by officers. The strange procession moved on to Nickleby's, then around the corner and down the alley to the motel. The group followed her to the door of Room 103.

The police took off her ropes and handcuffs and gave her a white, unclothed mannequin. Do to this what you said you did to Jamie, they told her.

She would later say that soon after they pulled open the thin blue door to Room 103, she felt a surge of relief.

"The measurements were different from the picture I had from my confession, the lighting, the doors, the floor jamb in between the bathroom and the little foyer hallway area. Everything was different," she recalled.

She said that up until that moment, a tiny part of her believed she might have killed Jamie, but when the reality of Room 103 did not match what she had seen in her mind's eye in the Ramada interrogation, "[a]ny doubts I had . . . [as far as] did this or didn't this happen was cemented. I did not kill Jamie."

Whatever relief she experienced, Kenzi continued with the "guilty" reenactment, albeit warily.

"I honestly told them, 'I'm either going to have to read the confession or you are going to have to explain to me where I should be standing when because I don't remember it any more,' " she recalled.

The police complied, telling her where to stand as she mimicked kissing Jamie, hitting her and stomping on her. The snapshots the police took, including those of her simulating oral sex on the mannequin and raising her foot above its neck, became part of the official court record. True to their word, the police also let her reenact the version in which she left Jamie safely showering and went to bed.

On the wintry morning Kenzi Snider reenacted her confession, she could not have grasped the subtleties of Korean law. She first met with her lawyer that afternoon. He had been hired by her mother at the recommendation of a friend in Thailand. Although people told them he was well-regarded, he spoke no English, and she returned to jail that night knowing little about her prospects.

In jail, she spent about twenty-three hours of every day in her cell. On Tuesdays and Fridays, guards escorted her to a communal bathroom for a twenty-minute shower. On other weekdays, she was allowed thirty minutes of recreation in the yard. She could see visitors for seven minutes a day except Sundays, when there were no visiting hours.

Her mother left her teaching job in Thailand to be near her. She had very little money and depended on charity to pay her rent. A friend from the family's days in Kuwait put her in touch with an Assemblies of God church, and its Korean congregants and pastor provided financial and moral support. They visited Kenzi in jail and found her pleasant and engaging despite her circumstances. She passed her days reading books the visitors brought and trying to make sense of the prison world she glimpsed in the recreation yard and on the marches to the shower room.

"It was hard to figure out how the jail worked because I didn't have anyone to show me. I didn't know at first that you couldn't go to bed until a certain time or that you had to wrap up your blankets," she recalled.

From stilted conversations with a guard trying to learn English, she discovered the prison was organized by a complicated code of colors and numbers. Inmates answered to the numbers on a tag on the left breast pocket of their uniforms. Kenzi was "4297." The color of the tags signified their crimes. Red was for fraud or embezzlement. Blue for drugs. Hers was yellow for murder. Inmates who already had been sentenced wore gray uniforms, while those awaiting trial wore pea green. To and from court and in front of a judge, they wore long heavy ropes knotted elaborately at their arms and looped around their backs. The ropes also were color-coded, and Kenzi quickly learned that they were more about shaming than protection. Dangerous prisoners were also handcuffed. On Kenzi, a murder suspect, guards used two sets of handcuffs under the ropes.

When her lawyer visited her, he brought his daughter, who knew a little English, and in their seven-minute meetings he tried to explain the trial process. It bore only a vague resemblance to a U.S. proceeding. Like many Asian countries, Korea has no jury system and trials are largely conducted on paper. The sort of public display that distinguishes the American system—crying witnesses, impassioned summations, contentious cross-examinations—are anathema to Korea's societal code of public propriety, respect and order.

In a Korean case, each side submits evidence in neat binders to a panel of judges. Witness accounts, forensic analysis, and legal accounts are also delivered in text form. At this stage, there are no arguments. About once a month, the lawyers and defendant appear before a panel of judges, who might ask for more paperwork, indicate which way they are leaning, or on rare occasions hear testimony from a witness whose account is disputed. After an undetermined number of these appearances, the judges issue a verdict.

Her first appearance was scheduled for March. In mid-February, a prison trustee appeared at her cell and asked for her uniform shirt. A few minutes later, she returned with the shirt and a smile. The number tag had been changed from yellow to white. "White good," the trustee managed in English.

The murder charge had been dropped and replaced with a count of assault with grievous bodily injury. The Korean murder statute required the offender to have demonstrated intention or malice when he killed. After some study of translations of her confession, prosecutors had determined that her account of striking Jamie in a panic did not show intent or malice. The downgrade meant Kenzi faced seven years in prison instead of the death penalty.

The change also meant Kenzi could enter the general prison population. From her cell in solitary confinement, she was moved to a fifteen-by-ten-foot room occupied by seven other women. In some ways, it was like settling into a new international school.

Figure out the dynamic, make friends, smile a lot. The women taught her some Korean and marveled over her willingness to learn their language and culture. They stared at her as she used her chopsticks to tuck into the simple rice and fish dishes.

The pastor from the Assemblies of God church brought her a bilingual Bible. The left-hand pages had the verses in Korean, while the right-hand pages had verses in English. Over time, the Bible became the cell's interpreter. If a Korean inmate was feeling hopeless, concerned about family, happy, scared or any other emotion, she would point out a Bible passage that expressed that sentiment and Kenzi would read its English translation. Her cellmates knew she had once worn a yellow tag, but they did not mention it, and she didn't ask them about their offenses.

When she did appear in court, Lee was there in the gallery monitoring the case's progress. Occasionally, he ran into her mother at the U.S. embassy and from time to time gave her a ride to court. He realized that it would probably seem strange to other investigators, but he felt it was the right thing to do. They were both Americans in a foreign country, and she was open about her financial situation.

"She was such a nice lady. She was so poor, though, and she asked me for advice about the cheap places to stay," he remembered.

He knew she could do without having to pay one thousand won for a subway ride. If I'm driving in that direction, I might as well take her, he thought.

In the car, Heath and Lee talked about the weather and the city and their families. Her son Durham was getting married. His mother was visiting from the

States. Lee was struck by Heath's enthusiasm and ef-
fusiveness. She loved to talk about the family's experiences living abroad, and her two favorite words were
"neat" and "terrific." It was clear where Kenzi had gotten her upbeat personality. It made for pleasant chats,
but Lee couldn't help but feel they were somehow odd.
How could she be so breezy when her only daughter
was in so much jeopardy? It just did not seem normal
to him.

CHAPTER 21

THREE BITES OF TOFU

When Patty Penich first learned that Kenzi was going to be sent to Korea to face charges, she was ecstatic. She imagined that the country had tougher laws, stricter judges and fewer opportunities for suspects to get off on technicalities than in the United States. The death penalty was carried out by hanging, not lethal injection, and that helped somewhat to alleviate her grief. She told reporters soon after Kenzi's arrest, "We won't have closure until she's swinging from the gallows. We want her to die the same way as Jamie."

The Korean system was not what Jamie's family had expected. The paper trials made it impossible for them to watch their daughter's case in person. Tickets to Seoul cost more than $1,000, hardly justifiable for a fifteen-minute hearing in which a judge might only say, "File more paperwork and come back in a month." They had to rely on third-hand accounts from the U.S. embassy staff and reporters from *Stars and Stripes* and the Associated Press.

And to Jamie's family, the prosecutors' decision to drop the capital murder charge seemed mindless and cruel. Someone had stomped the life out of Jamie with the sole of a boot. If that's not murder, they wondered what was.

Despite the disappointments, the Penichs remained focused on getting a guilty verdict. As the snow on Jamie's grave melted for a second spring, they told each other that a conviction was a conviction, whether for grievous bodily harm or murder. It held Kenzi Snider responsible for taking their girl's life. Enough time had passed that they knew vengeance would bring them no comfort, but a measure of justice, however small, would honor Jamie by acknowledging officially that her life had been stolen from her and that it wasn't fair or right.

What the Penichs did not detect in Derry as the days became longer and warmer was that a small section of the Korean criminal code was already unraveling their expectations for justice.

The issue was Kenzi's confession. In the United States, incriminating statements made to police officers are generally admissible at trial. When the suspect is in police custody and cannot just get up and walk away from the questions, detectives must give the Miranda warning, but if the suspect waives his rights or talks to officers when he is not in custody, the officers normally are permitted to testify about those statements.

In Korea, the rules are different. The society has an ambivalent relationship with confessions. On one hand, they are the cornerstones of its justice system. As many as ninety out of one hundred crimes are solved when the perpetrator confesses. Taking responsibility for one's action is ingrained in the culture. To lie or refuse to answer is to bring shame on one's family, a deeper shame perhaps even than going to prison.

On the other hand, history has given the Korean people a deep-seated distrust of police and authoritarian tactics in general. The Japanese conquered Korea in the early twentieth century and occupied it until the end of World War II. The police force was made up of Japanese and their Korean collaborators, and they kept order through terror. People suspected of working for the underground were beaten until they signed whatever confession the police put before them. During military rule in the 1970s and 1980s, antigovernment activists were similarly tortured in police custody into admitting all sorts of wrongdoing.

While this sort of abuse would have been devastating to any country, it was especially dangerous for a people so accepting of, and in fact encouraging of, legitimate confessions. As a result, the criminal justice code was written with safeguards against coerced confessions. Suspects who made incriminating statements to police officers in the backroom of a stationhouse had to repeat their confession in the light of day to a prosecutor. The rule reflected a Korean stereotype that had grown out of the nation's history: Police officers are oafish, violent and uneducated, while prosecutors, the cream of the law school crop, are learned Confucian gentlemen who would never stoop to brutality.

If a suspect who had confessed to police told a prosecutor the confession was false, it was as if the incriminating account never left his mouth. The prosecutor had to take the defendant's words over the police officer's, and the statement could not be admitted in court.

When Lee and Mansfield flew to West Virginia to interview Kenzi, they did not know about this wrinkle in the Korean system. When Lee was told about the statute in the spring of 2003, he was disturbed. Kenzi's confession relieved the pressure from the Penichs, Senator Specter, the Korean government and the embassy. Without it, they had no case. Lee knew that somehow he had to get her to reiterate her statement to a Korean prosecutor.

That spring, he summoned her to several meetings in the prosecutor's office in hopes of persuading her to repeat the confession. Kenzi's communication barrier with her own attorney left her in the dark about the statute, and the meetings with Lee and the prosecutors struck her as odd and pointless.

Sitting across the table from Kenzi, Lee asked her again and again to tell the prosecutor at the table what she had told him and Mansfield in the Ramada. Politely but firmly, she refused.

"I could tell he was frustrated, but I didn't know why he was that frustrated," Kenzi recalled.

Lee was persistent in the meetings.

"Come on, Kenzi, you know it's the truth. Tell him what you told me," he said.

Kenzi would bow slightly to the prosecutor, smile

and tell Lee apologetically that she could not swear to
something that was not true.

To Lee, the circular conversations were surreal and
underscored her guilt.

"All these times were opportunities for Kenzi to express her outrage, but she never did. She was always
very cordial. She said, 'Mr. Lee, I don't want to be rude,
but I can't agree with you.' How bizarre is that? She's
21, I'm accusing her of murder and she's saying, 'I don't
want to make you upset, Mr. Lee,'" he recalled.

If she's really innocent, he thought, *she would be
screaming from the rooftops. She would be coarse and
angry and tell him that he was ruining her life, but
there she sat smiling and apologizing.* He thought back
to the motel room in West Virginia and the moment
when Kenzi had left the room and then came back,
even though she was free to go.

"What made her come back was that she wanted to
convince us that she was a good person, that she hadn't
done this. That is somehow very important to her," he
thought.

What Lee found most frustrating was how unneces-
sary it all seemed. In three years in Seoul, he'd learned
that Koreans and Americans had vastly different views
on punishment. In America, long jail terms were proof
of society's disapproval, but in Korea, the emphasis
was on remorse and financial compensation. Defendants usually groveled for forgiveness and paid the
victims' family a large settlement before a case even
went before a judge. The shame was great, but the re-
sulting prison sentences were short—a few years for
murder, months for assault.

During their meetings, Lee noted these differences

again and again. Look, he told her, they don't care about jail time. They just care about you admitting what you did and making recompense to the victim's family. And since Jamie's family isn't here, they don't even care about that, he told her.

"This crime, not confessing to it is eating you alive, Kenzi. And for what? I can understand if you were trying to avoid the death penalty, but that's not the case anymore," he said.

"If you repeat the confession, you're only looking at about 3½ years more in prison with the time you've already served," he said. "I know you were telling us the truth in West Virginia. Why not let it out and be true to yourself? Pay the price and be done with it."

In one of their meetings, Lee told her that if she continued to maintain her innocence, the judges would focus on her lack of remorse and she would end up serving twenty-five years in prison. Kenzi would later say that it was the lowest moment in the entire ordeal.

"I don't care if I have to spend the rest of my life in prison. I am not going to admit to something I didn't do," she told him.

Lee stared at her. *You're crazy*, he thought. *I was there in West Virginia. I know you did it.*

The four judges in Seoul District Court wore coal-colored robes, identical silver ties and impassive expressions. They stared down from their long wooden bench at Kenzi Snider, who stood before them wearing a pea green uniform, heavy ropes and her blond hair pulled into a ponytail.

It was March 6, 2003, the first day of her trial, and

she was formally denying her confession in front of the judges and the prosecutors. Through an interpreter she said she had left Jamie Penich alive and preparing for a shower in the bathroom of Room 103. She said her confession was the result of pressure from the American investigators. She said she tried to maintain her innocence, but they "kept telling me I was wrong."

I did not kill her, she told them.

Lee listened in the spectators' gallery. That's it, he said. There would be no more meetings with Kenzi, no more attempts to get her to confess. She has made it official.

The judges reminded the prosecutors of the confession statute and adjourned the hearing until the next month. Like Lee, the prosecutors knew that without the confession there was little hope for conviction. There was no other evidence against Kenzi. After court, the prosecutors told Lee that they were going to take the unusual step of calling both him and Mansfield as witnesses. Their only option was a long shot. They would try to convince the judges that the American investigators, by virtue of their training and responsibilities, were the equivalent of Korean prosecutors, and that therefore Kenzi's confession should be admissible.

On May 1, Lee appeared before the judges and described the confession in the Ramada. The panel pressed him on whether he had permission from a prosecutor to conduct the interview, a common occurrence in Korea. No, he told them. Did you read the woman her rights, they asked. No, it was not a custodial interview, he said.

Lee was frustrated that neither the judges nor the prosecutors had asked him about Kenzi's allegations of coercion.

"I was going to explain to the judge how she had an opportunity to leave at any time and in fact did so, that she wasn't beaten up," he said.

He also wanted to tell them that suspects' fears were different in Korea than in America. Despite what they might see in Hollywood movies, the police did not beat up suspects in the States. It was not a legitimate concern the way it would be in Seoul, he believed. He wanted to tell the judges that while Korean suspects might assume they were going to be tortured or slapped around or intimidated or whatever, Kenzi would never have had that expectation.

Three weeks later, Mansfield flew in from his new posting at Fort Leavenworth, Kansas. His testimony, given through an interpreter, was tightly controlled by prosecutors to portray the confession as voluntary and as straightforward as possible. There was no mention of theme development or repression or any of the nuances of his testimony before Magistrate Taylor in Huntington.

"Kenzi suddenly shouted she committed murder and asked if she can go out to make a telephone call, and you allowed it. Is this correct?" the prosecutor asked, according to an Associated Press report.

"Yes," Mansfield said.

Asked what happened next, Mansfield said, "We asked her to sit, and she subsequently confessed."

On June 5, prosecutors made their final pitch to the judges. They went over the details of the confession and then asked for a sentence of seven years, much less than the twenty-five-year horror scenario Lee had painted for Kenzi.

The judges said they would mull the evidence and deliver the verdict in a couple of weeks.

The period in which they deliberated was no ordinary one in the Korean judicial world. The entire legal community was still reeling from the scandal of a hit man murdered during an interrogation by prosecutors.

The circumstances of his death were fodder for endless news stories. The dead man, Cho Cheon-hun, was reportedly beaten in the head with a police bat a foot and a half long. An accomplice told investigators the prosecutor and his assistants had used water torture on him to get a confession. The prosecutor and his investigators were going on trial. The victims' family was suing them. The president, Kim Dae-jung, who himself had been a victim of police torture in the 1980s, was outraged. The justice minister and the top prosecutor resigned, and the government announced it would close the interrogation rooms in the prosecutor's offices to prevent beatings.

In Korean society, the involvement of a prosecutor and his staff in brutality was stunning. A brutish unschooled police officer was one thing, but what chance was there for justice if the intellectual elite stooped to such tactics? Among judges, there was no greater topic of conversation. If the justice system refused to accept contested confessions, maybe police and prosecutors would stop beating suspects.

It was in this atmosphere that the judges reached their decision. On June 19, the four filed into their courtroom to announce their verdict. Guards led Kenzi into the well of the court. In the gallery behind her, her mother and pastor sat near Lee. As the lead judge, Justice Kim Nam-tae, began speaking, an interpreter whispered the English translation into her ear. They had no choice, the judge said, but to throw out the confession. Korean law requires it for the good of society. Without Kenzi's confession, Nam-tae said, "there is no other evidence to find her guilty of the alleged crimes. She is not guilty."

"Oh my God," her mother whispered. Kenzi struggled not to cry. She was told any public display of emotion would embarrass the judges. She bowed to the judges. Her mother stood up and tried to hug her daughter, but the pastor and others quickly instructed her to sit down. That is not proper, they told her. As the judges left the bench, Lee tried to slip out of the courtroom.

What's your reaction? a reporter asked.

"I have no comment," he stammered. He had held out hope that the court would find a way to hold Kenzi responsible. He was already thinking of the Penichs and how they would take the news.

Word of the acquittal arrived in Derry in the middle of the night, just as the news of Jamie's death had more than two years before. The family was stunned.

"It's a shock. We're very disappointed," Patty Penich managed to tell the Associated Press reporter who phoned.

Later that day, Kenzi walked out of the prison gates carrying a small bag of belongings. She had been incarcerated, either in the United States or Korea, for fifteen months.

"It's justice," she said, embracing her mother. "I feel really good."

On the advice of Korean friends, Heath Bozonie had come prepared with the ingredients of a traditional ritual. Kenzi sprinkled herself with salt, ate three bites of tofu and stepped on an egg. The ritual, she was told, would prevent a return to jail. And that was no small concern.

As she learned just after the acquittal, her freedom was far from assured. In Korea, unlike in the United States, prosecutors have the right to appeal an acquittal to a higher court and then to Korea's Supreme Court. In the moments right after the judges pronounced her not guilty, she had imagined being back in Minnesota for her twenty-second birthday on July 8. She imagined enrolling in classes at Marshall that autumn. But a week later, prosecutors announced they were going to try again.

It was something for the Penichs to cling to.

"It gives us a lot of hope," Patty Penich told a reporter.

Kenzi was told she would have to remain in Korea pending the appellate court's verdict. She told people, in true Snider fashion, that she planned to make the best of the time. Her brief time as an exchange student had not given her much of an opportunity to see the country. I will be a tourist, she said.

At first it was great to be free, but after the novelty wore off, she began to feel that she was still in a type of prison. She was not permitted to work and had little money. A church group had set up her and her mother in an apartment forty-five minutes outside Seoul. To show her gratitude to the church, she did some English tutoring, but at most that occupied a morning or two a week. The days were long and amorphous. The appellate court process was taking months. She went online and looked for friends in expat chat rooms. She went to bars and struck up conversation with Americans, many of them soldiers. They invited her to use the base's movie theater, pool and gym. Whenever they asked why she was in Korea, she hesitated before replying, "It's a long story."

She often ran into Agent Lee in the embassy, where she went to fill out paperwork. They were cordial to each other.

"I think he's an honorable man. I don't think he realizes what they did to me," she told people.

Lee watched Kenzi with her mother. *They are always so upbeat, always so playful, like teenage buddies more than parent and child,* he thought. He still thought of Kenzi as a good person, although one who had failed to do the right thing. One time, a relative brought him a box of oranges from a family farm. He saw Kenzi and Heath in the embassy and gave them half the box.

Often, Kenzi returned to Itaewon. Jamie's death still haunted her. Anything remotely connected to the murder, a song that had been playing in Nickleby's or the mention of St. Patrick's Day, filled her head with the image of Jamie's bloody, naked body.

"I wouldn't be okay for days," she recalled.

Her mother had trained her to define a problem and come up with solutions for it, and she set about trying to find a way to exorcise the ghosts. She went to Itaewon and walked the path she had taken that night. She says the trips made her see Itaewon as just a neighborhood with people and traffic, and Nickleby's as simply a pub. The Kum Sung is just a motel with beds and a shower, she said.

"Now, I can see the way it really is," she said. "Just memories."

She could walk down the alley where she and Jamie had walked and wave to kids peeking out from the doorways. She could stand at the entrance of Nickleby's, now transformed into a Mexican restaurant. She could laugh at the rowdy soldiers spilling out of bars.

"I feel sorry for the others," she said, referring to the exchange students. "They are still scared of this place, but I am not."

CHAPTER 22

US AND NOT US

On October 17, 2003, six months after Kenzi Snider's acquittal, the appellate court announced that its review of the case was complete and the three-judge panel was ready to issue a verdict.

Accompanied by her mother, Kenzi took an hour subway ride to the Seoul High Court's sprawling campus south of the Han River. The overcast, humid day seemed to reflect her mental state. As she trudged up the steep hill toward the modern, imposing court building, she looked down at her mauve sweater and realized that she might be wearing a prison uniform by nightfall.

A Korean law firm run by an American had agreed to handle Kenzi's appeal for free, and its attorneys assured her that the appellate verdict should be the same as that of the lower court. Despite a request from the judges for more evidence, the prosecutors had not added anything to the case file. They brushed off reporters' calls about the case, and the consensus around the courthouse seemed to be that they regarded the matter as an American mess dumped into the laps of Koreans.

It was the first time Kenzi had walked in the front door of a Korean courthouse. On her other trips, guards brought her in a back door, cuffed and wrapped in ropes. As she walked to the courtroom, she noticed how different the Korean system was from the U.S. system.

Security, an obsession of U.S. courts, is nonexistent, perhaps because personal handguns are banned in Korea. Lawyers, witnesses and employees enter and exit the buildings unimpeded. There are no metal detectors. Bags, briefcases and boxes are not screened.

Hallways in American courthouses are frequently loud and crowded, seeming to double as recovery rooms, cafeterias and day cares. In Korea, they are clean, silent and empty, save for clerks who walked swiftly and silently between offices carrying stacks of folders. Relatives of the victims and defendants rarely come to court.

The courtroom where Kenzi's case was to be decided was almost comically ornate. Crimson and midnight velvet trimmed the walls and the chairs. An enormous crystal chandelier bathed the room in a soft yellow light that seemed more appropriate for a dinner party than a legal proceeding. The judges wore dramatic purple and black.

It was sentencing day, and guards escorted prisoners

from a rear holding cell into the court. Four months had passed since Kenzi first saw the color-coded uniforms and the heavy ropes. As the lead judge pronounced each sentence, the prisoner stared at the floor, then bowed to the judges and was led out.

Finally, her name was called. She rose and walked into the well, her lawyer on one side and an interpreter on the other. The lead judge, Justice Jun Bong-jin, delivered the decision: The confession was inadmissible. Beyond that, he said, the evidence suggested that someone else had killed Jamie Penich. In a soft-spoken, steady voice, the judge ticked off a list of evidence pointing toward a male perpetrator. Among them: the man with the bloody pants seen by the motel manager's wife, the angry American male voice a fellow student had heard, and the lack of blood on Kenzi's clothes and shoes.

"It is very reasonable the person who committed this crime might be a third person, not Miss Snider," he said.

When he finished, Kenzi bowed slightly and returned to the gallery, where she collapsed in her mother's arms, crying. She allowed herself a few minutes of relief before reminding herself and her mother that she still had one more hurdle. There was no doubt prosecutors would appeal to the Supreme Court.

"I'm saving my emotions for the very end, when it will all be over. Until then, it's like, 'Don't get too excited,'" she told a few reporters who were on hand for the verdict.

An hour later, an embassy official called the Penichs. The family had braced for the decision.

"Of course, we're upset, but we were expecting it,"

Patty said. She was trying to sound resigned, but anger simmered under her words.

"The way their system is set up is just terrible. She's going to get off, and they're just going through the motions," she said.

Shortly after the verdict, Heath Bozonie packed up her things and flew to Minnesota, leaving Kenzi on her own. The wedding of her middle son, Durham, was set for the end of December, and she was needed to make the bridesmaids' dresses.

Kenzi was eager to follow. Her lawyers petitioned the prosecutors for her to return to Minnesota for the wedding. After all the formality of the Korean courts, it was a very casual agreement. The prosecutors, exhausted from a politically charged American case that they seemed not to want, asked her if she would return if the Supreme Court found her guilty. She promised she would.

Okay, you can go, they told her. The lead prosecutor handed back her passport and a Post-it with his cell phone number in case there was a problem at the airport. When she asked for something more official, a consular officer at the U.S. embassy e-mailed a two-paragraph letter to her Hotmail account.

On Christmas Day 2003, almost a year to the date that she'd arrived in handcuffs, Kenzi flew to Minnesota. She made it in time for her brother's wedding. For the Penichs, her return had a special cruelty. Jamie's older sister, Jennell, also was getting married, but Jamie wouldn't be there.

Later that year, both Kenzi and the Penichs cooperated with a piece on the case on the ABC newsmagazine *Prime Time Live*. In the piece, the Penichs made it clear that they believed Kenzi had killed their daughter and gotten away with murder.

Shortly after the program aired, the Penichs got a call from a woman with an accent. She said she was Portuguese and had seen the show.

"All I can tell you is check the bear, check the bear," she told Brian Penich. He was confused, and the woman hung up before he could get any more information.

Was she referring to one of the soldier suspects, Nick Baer? the family wondered. Baer's name was never mentioned in the piece, or in any story ever published.

At the kitchen table, Jennell and Amanda told Patty to just forget about it. Just let it go, mom, they said. Patty felt she should tell someone. With Mansfield gone, she passed the information to the CID agent who had replaced him in Seoul. She said she and Brian still were certain that Kenzi had killed their daughter, but they suspected Baer was somehow involved.

The agent seemed hesitant.

Technically, he said, the case was closed when Kenzi was arrested.

"He said that he'd have to check with his superiors before he could contact Nick Baer," she recalled. "I got the feeling he was humoring me."

While they spoke, the agent told Patty that in their office on MP Hill, they kept a photo of Jamie to remind them that perseverance in an investigation paid off. From Patty's perspective, there was not much of a payoff. The woman who confessed to killing her daughter was free and the man she believed an accomplice had never served a day in jail. But as the months and years passed, she was grateful if anyone outside their family remembered Jamie at all.

"I thanked him for that," she recalled.

A year passed and then another, and Kenzi Snider's guilt remained an open issue before the Supreme Court of Korea. It was very unusual for the justices to take so long to rule, but few in Seoul's legal circles could blame them for foot dragging. This case is a headache, those familiar with the court's workings said. An American case, botched by Americans, what good will come out of ruling either way? If they acquit her, the Americans will be angry. But how can they convict her under our law?

Since Kenzi's first trial, the law governing confessions had become even more of a problem for prosecutors. In the wake of the accused hit man's death at the hands of prosecutors, the courts in Korea raised the bar for confessions. In most cases, it was no longer enough for a prosecutor to hear an incriminating statement from a suspect. If the suspect denied the confession to a judge, it was as if it never happened. The long-shot argument the prosecutors had put forth—that the FBI and army agents were the equivalent of prosecutors— was moot. Acquittal seemed the only real possibility, but the justices were silent.

In Seoul, Jamie Penich's name is most often met with quizzical looks. Even reporters, police officials and prosecutors, the individuals that one would expect to recall such a tragic murder of a young woman, seem to strain to place the name. Once in a while, someone remembers.

Oh yes, the person will say. The lesbian. Or no, she wasn't a lesbian, but the girl who killed her was. I forget. Wasn't someone a lesbian? Whatever happened with that case?

The short memories of Koreans does not surprise Dr. Kim. She left her administrative position shortly after Jamie's murder and is back teaching students about minorities in Korean society and the effect of mass media on the culture.

She struggles to explain why Jamie's case had little resonance for Koreans. It comes down to the Korean concept of inside and outside, she said. We are a very insular, homogeneous people and we tend to divide everything into what is us and what is not us, she explains. It's like a house. When you are outside, you wear your shoes and you show a hard demeanor, but when you are inside, you take off your shoes and relax. A murder involving Americans in Itaewon, that is outside the house, she says.

"Maybe if she was here longer and she had gotten to know people, then maybe it would be different. But she was only here for two weeks," she says.

Itaewon remains a party zone, but there are fewer Americans. The U.S. military is in the process of moving out of the Yongsan Garrison to a new base south of the city. By 2008, the Americans will be gone and Korea will take over the sprawling base in the middle of the crowded city.

On weekends, soldiers still come to Hooker Hill, but they can no longer stay out all night. Just after the September 11 attacks, the military instituted a curfew. The base commanders also barred soldiers from visiting a long list of bars that encourage prostitution. On weekend nights, military policemen patrol the alleys of Itaewon enforcing the new rules.

Nickleby's has been redecorated as a Mexican cantina. The soldiers who partied there in 2001 are long gone. Their replacements, many of whom were in junior high school when Jamie died, have not heard of the murder.

"Wow, that's wild," they say when told about the case.

The men first considered suspects have moved on. Josh Harlan, the dental technician who kissed Jamie on the dance floor, left the army and returned to Montana, where he serves in the National Guard. Discussing the case five years later, he struggles to remember Jamie's first name. He says he has separated the long night he spent under CID interrogation from the rest of his time in Seoul.

"For me, Korea was great. I would do almost all of it over again," he says.

Michael Kolinski, the infantry captain who also kissed Jamie on the dance floor, finished his second year-long tour in Iraq in 2005. The war has faded many of his memories of Korea, but he says he still remembers drinking too much, running the hash and the CID officers who were so convinced he had killed a young woman he could barely recall.

"I didn't even know her last name," he says. "They had to tell me."

Vincent, the captain who hit on Kenzi in the bar booth, also served in Iraq, commanding a military intelligence unit protecting the Green Zone in Baghdad.

He is married now, and he and his wife run a toy drive through their church for Iraqi children. In an e-mail from Baghdad, he writes that he does not have much information to offer.

"Kenzi was just a girl that I hit on. Nothing more, nothing less. In my single days, I hit on lots of girls. I honestly do not remember her personality. If all this had not happened, I would have said, 'fun,' but I really don't remember much about her," he writes.

He says that when he found out about her arrest, "I was happy that the real killer had been found. A really crazy story had taken an unexpected turn."

He has lost touch with his friend Javier Martinez, who left the army and is living in California. Of the main suspects approached about the case, only Nick Baer declines to talk. He is a sergeant stationed at an army hospital in Virginia. He sent a letter to the hospital spokeswoman saying he didn't wish to discuss Jamie Penich.

Lee says he isn't surprised.

"I think his experience with the CID was more traumatic than any other suspect that came in," Lee says. "He was the most scrutinized."

Lee works at FBI headquarters, the J. Edgar Hoover Building in downtown D.C. He inspects field offices for the bureau, a step in the promotion ladder, he explains. It is not exciting, and he does not expect anything in his career could ever match the thrill of the Penich case.

"I'm still amazed even today that Kenzi confessed," he says.

"That particular day in West Virginia is the most memorable moment in my twenty-year bureau career.

It was an amazing experience I went through, and I appreciate it. I feel I witnessed something special. If you read the confession, it's like poetry. I'm just sorry she didn't have the maturity to see this all the way through," he says.

Lee bristles when asked about evidence that might indicate a male killer.

"The motel owner and Miss Yi and what the other student heard, we'd be sitting here trying to figure that out still today if Kenzi hadn't confessed. But she did, so it's meaningless," he says.

He adds, "The outcome of this case would seem to say something about the truth, but it actually doesn't say anything."

Mark Mansfield left the army in December 2003 and took a job as a civilian investigator for the CID office in Vicksburg, Mississippi. After Hurricane Katrina, much of his work related to detecting fraud in contracts given out by the Army Corps of Engineers. He moved his family to Mississippi, but he spends most of his time on the road traveling between construction projects. He has approached the assignment with the same zeal he brought to the Penich case. He works nights and weekends and worries that his family, which now includes a fourth child, a son, does not see him enough.

Reached on his cell phone on the Gulf Coast of Mississippi, he says that he wants to talk about his investigation, but that it is emotionally difficult.

"This thing is so close to my heart," he says.

His supervisors at CID headquarters insist all questions for Mansfield be submitted in writing. After months of negotiations, Mansfield's answers arrive by e-mail. He writes that he is proud of his investigation despite the result and feels sorry that some believe he was responding to political pressure when he targeted Kenzi.

"The fact that I felt no pressure from Mr. Specter's inquiry can be believed or not believed, but it is true. My career did not hinge on the case being solved or not," he writes.

He brushes off suggestions that he tried to coerce a confession from Michael Greco or Kenzi to close the case.

"To infer as much means that we didn't care about the truth in this investigation, and I personally spent too much of my life and energy on this investigation to merely settle for a fabricated confession and close the file," he writes.

He says he thinks of the case often and what he might have done differently. He wishes they had done more to try to find the boots that Kenzi wore the night of the murder. The boots could have been the smoking gun, he suggests.

"For the clothes she was wearing that evening to have been so readily available to her, I don't like the way the boots have just vanished," he writes.

As part of Jamie's memorial service, the University of Pittsburgh planted a purple beech tree in the yard of Heinz Chapel. The university was supposed to mark the tree with a plaque, but five years later, it has yet to be erected, and the lack of marker makes it difficult to locate the tree. Officials from the public affairs office make several phone calls and a couple of field trips to the yard. Eventually, they identify a tree that seems to be Jamie's beech. It is the right size, neither a sapling nor old wood, a sort of adolescent of trees. It stands near a sidewalk. On weekdays, students trudge by it on their way to class. On weekends, wedding parties sweep by it on their way up the chapel stairs.

Just down Fifth Avenue is the study-abroad office. It is a bright, busy place. Large windows bathe under-graduates in sunlight as they read colorful pamphlets about exchange programs in Paris and Tokyo and Sydney. The students seem uniformly gleeful.

For a time after the murder, Jamie's picture hung in the reading room. As time went by, however, fewer people knew Jamie or her story. Eventually, the photo came down. In her office down the hall, Angi Yucas remembers how she and a colleague used to send the Penichs flowers on the anniversary of Jamie's death. After a couple of years, they wondered if it was more upsetting than helpful and stopped. Dr. Yucas keeps a file on Jamie in the cabinet by her desk, but she rarely looks at it. Paging through the folder remains a draining experience. Her eyes well with tears when she thinks about that raw spring. Since then, she has dealt with some date rapes and terrorism fears, but nothing compares to Brian Penich's cracking voice asking her to "just bring her home." She is glad she went to the viewing and the funeral. She remembers the words of the grief counselor.

"Nothing we can do can really take away the pain. All you can do is try to assure the parents that their child will be remembered," she echoes.

Jamie's fiancé, Jeff Gretz, still lives in Pittsburgh, but

he is often on tour as a drummer in a metal band named Zao. Twice he agrees to talk about Jamie, only to cancel. Her parents no longer have contact with him.

"He's doing his thing and that's fine," Patty Penich says.

Mia Scott Shea, Jamie's roommate and best friend, married and moved to Sacramento. For a week after Jamie's death, she stayed with the Penichs, but as the months stretched on, she found her contact with them more and more difficult. There was nothing that she could say or do to ease their pain, and she wondered if the developments in her life—graduation, marriage— served only as unpleasant reminders of the life Jamie would never have.

"I think about Jamie every day," she says before asking how the Penichs are doing.

"Tell them that I think about them too," she adds.

In Derry, change is slow and subtle. A new priest. One less business in town. Another row in the cemetery. A decade has passed since Jamie left the high school on Chestnut Street, and the teenagers who hurtle through the halls each day may not recognize her name. The teachers, the keepers of all institutional knowledge, remember Jamie, though. Sometimes, it's seeing Patty or Brian in town that makes them think of her. Other times, it's the echo of her personality in a current student. They see a quiet, self-assured young woman who casts her eyes not on the hills around town, but over them. It is these kids, the Jamies, that delight and terrify them.

"I think that with the children that we love, when

they want to experience life, all we can do is pray that in that ride of experience, life doesn't get taken from them," Jamie's English teacher, Linda Warner, says. "Unfortunately, that is what happened to Jamie."

Some of Jamie's classmates eventually left Derry to find work or to marry, but many of them eventually returned. There is just something in Derry, they say. No place else feels like home. One who left and returned is Jamie's high school boyfriend, Jason Young.

Married with two children, he inspects nuclear tubing at the Westinghouse plant in nearby Blairsville. Whenever he drives past St. Martin's, he thinks of Jamie in his passenger seat, crossing herself. He notes the spot across the street where he stood when they carried her casket into the church. He sometimes sees her parents in town, but he finds himself avoiding them. Other than a whispered "sorry" at the viewing, he has not spoken to Patty or Brian. The conversation he had with Jamie just before she left for her senior year abroad haunts him. She was going to chicken out and stay in Derry, but he would not let her.

"It's stupid, I guess, but I just feel guilty. Like I could've talked her out of going to Belgium and then maybe she never would've gone to Korea," he says.

When people ask how many children they have, Brian and Patty always say three. They talk about Jamie in the present tense. Jamie likes her grandmother's spaghetti. Jamie loves tennis. Jamie wants to see the world. Patty tells people that she keeps sane by pretending that Jamie is just away at school, gone on some wild international trip.

"Jamie's at school, Jamie's traveling," she says, flinging her hand out toward the picture window in her living room.

She smiles, but there is a distinct bitterness in it. The truth is that every moment of every day the Penichs are aware their daughter is dead. They have learned to walk around the hole in their lives rather than flinging themselves into it as they did for the first few months, but it is still there, gaping.

Brian, the more emotional of the two, has difficulty even saying his daughter's name to a stranger. Patty can seem hardened, but her grief is raw and just beneath the surface. She still carries Jamie's flight itinerary in her wallet. They were standing in the Pittsburgh airport and Jamie just wanted to get on the plane and go, but Patty made her write down on this little scrap of paper the flight number, the time and the date: June 11, 2001. It is like the deed to a house destroyed by a flood, proof that she had something once and it was ripped away from her lawlessly.

"I'll probably never take it out," she says.

The Penichs' mourning breaks into chapters. There was their initial, all-consuming sadness when Patty couldn't get out of bed and they didn't open their mouths except to sob. Then there was the investigation, the desperate search for answers that gave them a sense of purpose and therefore hope. There was the rage they felt toward Kenzi after the confession. That gave way to bitter disappointment when she was acquitted.

In the years since then, they have learned to manage that heartbreak. They eventually gathered the strength to pack up Jamie's room. She impressed them to the end. They shook their heads at the anthropology books that filled her shelves.

"How did she read this stuff?" they asked each other.

They found they could still experience moments of great joy. Jennell got married. Amanda graduated from high school. Brian turned fifty, and Patty threw him a big party at the firehouse. They survived more heartbreak when Jennell miscarried her first child.

Throughout all the developments, they kept Jamie in their thoughts and conversations. But during a busy winter week a few years after her murder, a handful of days passed without the mention of her name. Jennell, rushing through the grocery checkout, handed the clerk a club card. The store employee paused.

"Are you Jamie Penich?" she asked.

Jennell was taken aback.

"Why are you asking me that?" she said.

The clerk pointed out that the card belonged to "Jamie L. Penich." Jennell had no idea how her sister's card had gotten in her wallet, but the family took it as a message.

"It was like Jamie saying to all of us, 'Don't forget about me. Please don't forget about me,'" she said.

St. Martin's cemetery spreads down a long, gentle hill behind the church. The small American flags that mark the graves of veterans seem to wave from every third stone. As the graveyard slopes down from the parking lot, the old, cracked headstones of nineteenth-century farmers give way to the modest family plots of coal miners of the 1950s and 1960s and eventually to the newer graves of factory workers and truckers.

At least twenty-nine members of the Penichs' extended family are buried there.

Jamie's grave is in the most recent section, a flat field at the bottom of the hill. It was once a woods where Patty and her best friend played as children. Jamie's grave stands out from twenty-five feet. It is covered in roses and stuffed animals. The largest decoration is a carved wooden angel. She has brown hair and is lying on her stomach reading a thick book.

The headstone is black and flush with the ground:

PENICH
Jamie Lynn
Sept. 19, 1979
March 17, 2001

If tears could build a stairway
and memories were a lane,
we'd walk right up to heaven
and bring you back again

Separating Jamie's family name and her first name, there is an engraving unique in St. Martin's cemetery. It is a map of the world. The Penichs might have selected something more traditional, praying hands, perhaps, or a simple cross or the lamb that is a favorite on the graves of children. But tradition never defined Jamie. Even if her family did not always understand Jamie's dreams, and even if her dreams took her away from them, they knew that it was those plans for the future that made Jamie who she was. It seemed right to acknowledge that on her headstone.

She wanted so desperately to get out of Derry and see

the world. For a brief time, she lived her dream, and then she had to come home. She is buried in a field that overlooks her hometown, surrounded by people who lived their entire lives in it. When Jennell's son died, the family comforted themselves with thoughts of Jamie caring for him. They buried the baby in Jamie's plot, on top of her casket.

When her parents die, her father will be buried on her left, and her mother on her right. "That way she will be with us forever," Patty explains.

Of all the places Jamie traveled and all the places she wanted to see, her mother says she feels certain her daughter's spirit is in Derry.

"She's here. She's in the house. It's peaceful here," Patty says.

Shortly after Kenzi's arrest, the Penichs filed preliminary paperwork for a civil suit against her. They see little point in pursuing it.

"To file a civil suit is to go after money. If Kenzi Snider has no money, there's no use," Patty says. "So we have to wait until Kenzi Snider makes something of herself."

When she mentions the woman she believes killed her daughter, it is always by first and last name, as if she is a concept rather than an actual person. Mostly though, she tries not to talk about her at all.

"I could probably find 20 ways to do away with Kenzi Snider and not think twice, but I feel nothing for her," she says.

CHAPTER 23

PRISON IN THE MIRROR

Hello, Yellow Cab, this is Kenzi. How may I help you?"

It's close to midnight on a Thursday, and Kenzi Snider is working the graveyard shift as a taxi dispatcher in St. Cloud. She balances the phone receiver on her shoulder and types addresses into a computer.

"402 33rd Ave North? Okay we'll get one over there for you. Five to fifteen. Okay, bye."

She says the cab company is the only job she could land when she returned to the United States two years ago. She filled out applications at the chain stores, but they never called back. In some cases, it seemed to her that background checks were flagging her as an accused murderer. In others, the interviewer asked about the gap of two years in her résumé. She explained as concisely as possible that she'd been accused of murder, held in prison for fifteen months, six of which were in a Korean jail, and had then been acquitted by two lower courts, but that she was technically still facing murder charges in the Korean Supreme Court. They never called her in for a second interview. Yellow Cab is owned by the stepfather of a friend. She makes $8.50 per hour. No benefits.

While in jail, she defaulted on her student loans, charge cards and phone bills. Her credit was ruined. She wanted to return to Marshall, get an education degree and go into teaching, but until she repays the thousands she owes in federal and state loans, she can't get financial aid anywhere.

"That is the hardest part, the coming back. People think you are out of prison, life's great, but you get your life smacked back at you like whiplash," she says.

She came back to St. Cloud because her mother and brothers are here, and the family still owns a house where she could live for free. She shares the two-story bungalow with her mother. It is dilapidated and messy. Broken toys are strewn about the screened-in front porch. A sewing machine sits on the living room coffee table. Documents related to the case are stacked in various piles. Some rooms are carefully decorated with mementoes from the family travels. Others are half painted Day-Glo colors. Heath Bozonie tells a visitor she is embarrassed by how the house looks.

"We're sort of in between," she says.

Kenzi's job makes for weird hours. She gets home at dawn and tries to sleep, but traffic and the phone interrupt her sleep. She says she is exhausted most of the time. When she was promoted from taking calls at the cab company to dispatching, she was offered a day shift, but she says she felt sorry for the graveyard dispatcher, a mother who wanted to be home while her kids slept, and so she took the overnight shift.

"She needed it more than I did," she says.

The work is not difficult, and she is grateful for any income, but sometimes it is hard not to get depressed. In the wee hours, the callers are often drunk or high and frequently impatient. A frustrated customer once screamed at her to "Get an education."

Kenzi laughed ruefully. If only you knew, she thought.

"It's not using the best of my talents," she says. She pauses, and then in Snider fashion adds, "but it's still something. I didn't know how to do this before."

Even if someone wrote her a check for tuition tomorrow and she didn't need to rely on student loans, Kenzi says she doesn't want to return to school or even leave Minnesota until the high court acquits her. She says she wants to hold the piece of paper in her hand, even if she cannot read the characters. It will be proof that this period of my life is over, she says.

She thinks that the verdict could come any day. The judges in Korea could stamp their decision while she is dispatching a cab or shopping for groceries or sleeping. Then and only then, she says, I can restart my life.

Her mother is eager for the verdict too. Her life is also on hold. She talks about getting another international school job and has applied for positions, but part of her wants to wait for Kenzi to get her life settled.

"They are in a holding pattern, and they have been for two years. They need to find a way to somehow go forward," her eldest brother, Jordan, says.

Kenzi's brothers and friends say they notice a distinct change in her personality since she returned from jail in Korea. She still has an easy laugh and a friendly manner, but they say they see something dark where there once was only light.

Erin Lambert, who went to high school in Kuwait with Kenzi and now lives in Minneapolis, says, "The Kenzi I knew in high school was never cynical. She's cynical now. She doesn't want to give people the opportunity to hurt her.

"The light in her eyes is just gone, and it doesn't seem like she's having fun even breathing," she says.

Kenzi has a handful of friends in St. Cloud. They hang out in the pubs and coffeehouses in the small downtown area. They know how to make her laugh, but in her mind, every day is just marking time until she can get out of town. At the taxi company, she stares out a small window that looks onto the darkened garage bay. Occasionally a bored taxi driver stops by to chat. They are older. St. Cloud is their home.

"Everybody in this town is kinda stuck here rather than wanting to be here," she says. "And a whole town of stuck people isn't the nicest."

She says she doesn't go to church because she hasn't found one she likes. She doesn't talk about God as much as in her jail days. She was always a little plump, but in the last couple of years, she has put on more weight.

"I feel like my whole life is on hold," she says.

Driving a visitor around St. Cloud in her used Volkswagen, she points out the major attractions. There's the university, the river, the history museum and a park. She says the most impressive thing is a little drive outside town. She drives down a winding, wood-lined road and makes a left. At the end of a small drive, a massive granite façade rises out of the forest like a gothic castle. A sign identifies it as the Minnesota State Corrections Facility—St. Cloud. The windows are tall and arched like a cathedral, but the bars on them clearly identify the place as a prison. The building is more than a hundred years old and surrounded by a wall twenty-two feet high and nearly five feet thick.

Kenzi drives slowly through the lot. She is explaining that on her nights off from the cab company, she often has trouble sleeping. Without work to distract her, she says, it is easy to get lonely and sad. She says that when she cannot sleep, she gets in her car and drives. More often than not, she says, she ends up here, in the parking lot of the prison.

She says she just sits in her car, crying. After a while, she says, she tries to buck herself up.

"I tell myself, 'At least I was only in jail and not a prison. At least I never had bars on the window,'" she says.

"I go there feeling sad, but I leave there feeling better. I was in jail for 15½ months, that could easily have been 15½ years," she adds.

After a moment, she turns out of the parking lot and heads back to town, the prison in her rearview mirror.

On Friday, January 13, 2006, the Supreme Court of South Korea acquitted Kenzi Snider of all charges in the death of Jamie Penich. Brian and Patty Penich learned of the verdict from a reporter.

"We never thought they would take her back to Korea," Patty said matter-of-factly.

Some judges in Korea could stamp any document they wanted and call it anything they wanted. It had nothing to do with the truth, Patty said.

"That little piece of paper does not mean squat," she added.

Kenzi's lawyer in Seoul delivered the news in a midnight phone call to the Snider home in St. Cloud. Kenzi, however, was not there. Despite her pledge to stay in Minnesota until the verdict, she had moved back to West Virginia several months earlier.

"It seemed like it was never going to happen, and I'd wasted two years of my life and I didn't want to waste any more," she explained.

Her overjoyed mother took the lawyer's message and quickly called her daughter's cell phone. Kenzi was in bed and ignored the first call, but when the phone kept ringing, she answered.

"My reaction was 'Wow.' A lot of 'wows,'" she said.

She called a few friends and sent some e-mails, but "it was too late to do anything really momentous," she said.

The next day, she teared up when someone sent her a bouquet of flowers. Overall, however, it struck her as anticlimactic. She had known what the verdict would be. It did not give her the future she wanted. She had wangled a job at a small store in the mall, but she still owed thousands in student loans. A return to classes was years away.

A few weeks later, a professor at Northwestern Law School, which has a center specializing in wrongful conviction cases, said the school's legal clinic would represent Kenzi in a potential civil suit. Although the professor declined to identify whom she might sue, the army and the FBI seemed likely targets. Kenzi, whose words had gotten her in so much trouble, seemed to have learned a lesson. She referred all questions about the matter to her lawyer.

AUTHOR'S NOTE

But did she do it?

Since I started reporting this case three years ago, I've gotten that question hundreds of times. It doesn't matter whether the person asking has just heard my three-minute condensed version shouted over the roar of a restaurant or has sat down and read the entire manuscript. At the end, the listener always wants me to tell him if I think Kenzi did it. The mind loves a puzzle, but only if it has a solution, it seems.

People seeking my opinion almost always go on to express their own. There is no consensus. Some are convinced she did it. Others think she is clearly innocent. But they are uniformly confident in their conclusions. What interests me, and I guess to some extent reassures me, is that the opinions are nearly always tied to a single piece of evidence. The lack of blood on her clothes, for example. That's all you need to know, I've been told. It's proof she didn't do it. Others will cite the man in the bloody pants. What more do you need, someone will say. It was a soldier. Others will hone in on Anneloes. There's no way the roommate slept through that. The cops need to get her in a motel room and ask her some tough questions, they'll say.

Those who believe Kenzi murdered Jamie point quite obviously to the confession. And within it, different people focus on different aspects. Some zero in on the level of detail. No one could just make that stuff up, they say. Others point to the bruise across Jamie's back. How could she know about that if she wasn't the one who dropped her? they say.

If I ask someone who believes Kenzi is innocent—perhaps someone who is persuaded by the lack of blood on her clothes—what he makes of a contradictory piece of evidence, perhaps the fact Jeroen only felt her crawl into bed once, he simply brushes it off. It doesn't matter because her jeans would've been bloody if she did it, he says.

It seems impossible to put all the evidence together at one time and develop a coherent picture. This is a case where the more one knows, the less certain one is. The only way to find an answer, it seems, is to cling to one tree and refuse to acknowledge the forest.

But did she do it?

Being impartial is foremost when I report on investigations and trials. I am careful never to express an opinion. What I think is irrelevant, I tell people who inquire. It's what the jury thinks that matters. I do have opinions, of course. I've seen all the evidence and know the players. It would be strange if I didn't lean one way or another, if I didn't think: "That man is guilty as sin" or "The DA didn't have any evidence."

But in this case, even if you put a gun to my head, I just couldn't tell you what happened in Room 103. Even after two trips to Korea, scores of interviews and repeated reviews of hundreds of pages of transcripts and documents, certainty remains elusive.

So did she do it?

I don't know. And that is the truth.